THE 48 HOUR

RELATIONSHIP RETREAT

YOUR STEP-BY-STEP GUIDE TO FINDING YOUR DREAMS AND PLANNING FOR SUCCESS TOGETHER
- IN ONE FABULOUS WEEKEND -

AMANDA ADAMS-BARNEY
RICHARD BARNEY

Love Your Life

LoveYourLife

Love Your Life Publishing
Wilmington, Delaware
www.loveyourlifepublishing.com

ISBN: 978-1-934509-71-5
Library of Congress Control Number: 2013944994

Printed in the United States of America
First Printing 2013

TABLE OF CONTENTS
(Finding the Stuff You Want)

INTRODUCTION (PRE-AMBLE) i

HOW WE'VE ORGANIZED THIS BOOK (WHATCHA GOT THERE?)
.... ix

SECTION 1 – MAKING THE CASE...xiii

Chapter 1 – How This Started (Let's Start at the Very Beginning/ It's a Very Good Place to Start)......................1

Chapter 2 – Answering the Critics (Okay, Doubting Thomas — Bring It ON!) 9

SECTION 2 – PREPARING FOR YOUR RETREAT 17

Chapter 3 – Time and Place (Hi Ho, Hi Ho! It's Off to Work You Go!) 21

Chapter 4 – The Agenda (Design on a Dime) 29

Chapter 5 – Ground Rules (Leveling the Playing Field) 41

Chapter 6 – Being Prepared (What to Expect When You're Expecting — a Retreat, That Is...) 51

INTERMISSION 55

Chapter 7 – Cuddle Break.. 59

SECTION 3 – THE WORKBOOK.. 61

Chapter 8 – Using the Workbook (What Are We Supposed to Do with This?)... 65

Chapter 9 – The Method for Working through Each Topic (As Tim Gunn Would Say, "Make it work!") 69

Chapter 10 – Beginning the Retreat (Ladies and Gentlemen, Start Your Engines) 79

Chapter 11 – Goals and Values (Are You Building on a Firm Foundation or on a Swamp?) 85

Chapter 12 – Relationship (Just You and Me) 95

Chapter 13 – Finances (Money Makes the World Go Round) 105

Chapter 14 – Careers (It's All in a Day's Work) 117

Chapter 15 – Spirituality (You Gotta Have Faith) 123

Chapter 16 – Health and Wellness (I Feel Good!) 131

Chapter 17 – Home (Our House...Is a Very, Very, Very Fine House) 139

Chapter 18 – Family (We Are Fam-i-ly) 149

Chapter 19 – Scheduling (I'm Late, I'm Late...for a Very Important Date) 161

Chapter 20 – Intimacy (We're Bringing Sexy Back) 169

Chapter 21 – Your Topic Here (That's Right — You're the Expert) 177

Chapter 22 – Budget Review (Please Stop the Pain!) 181

SECTION 4 – MAKING IT STICK...........................**185**

Chapter 23 – Making Plans (Time for Action, Jackson) 189

Chapter 24 – After the Retreat (Is the Party Really Over?) 195

SECTION 5 – OTHER STUFF **201**

Acknowledgements (A Big Heaping Helping of Thank Yous) 203

About the Authors 207

INTRODUCTION
(Pre-Amble)

INTRODUCTION
(Pre-Amble)

"Little ditty about Jack and Diane, two American kids growing up in the heartland...little ditty about Jack and Diane, two American kids doing the best they can." — John Cougar-Mellencamp

And that is what we are (though our names are Richard and Amanda) — two all-American kids who met at a comedy club in Washington, DC, dated for two years, got married, had our son, Joshua, five years after that, and our daughter, Carli, came into our lives four years later. We have survived seventeen years of marriage (and counting). Sure, there are some pretty unconventional things about us, but at the heart of it we are just two American kids doing the best we can.

DISCLAIMER: Our dilemma for the introduction is this: How many people actually read the introduction? Our bet is only the truly Type A's among us (our kin, BTW). Many folks want to cut right to the chase and skip over the introduction to get to the "good stuff."

So what do we put here? We decided on items that will give you overachievers a glimpse behind the curtain, and yet the slackers who skipped ahead won't miss anything important. Consider it a kind of reward for being so thorough.

So...what are your BIG benefits, you ask?

#1 — We'll tell you a little about ourselves so you have some context for our stories. (And if you really care, visit our website and you can put faces with the names.)

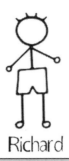 

Richard   Amanda

	Richard	Amanda
Married	17 years (but don't ask us our status after a particularly stressful weekend)	
Kids	Josh — 12; Carli — 9 (at least this week — we haven't sold them yet)	
Hometown	Missoula, MT	Pittsburgh, PA
Sports fans of	Miami Dolphins Washington Nationals Washington Capitals	Pittsburgh Steelers (big time) Washington Nationals Washington Capitals
Other sports we like to watch	Motocross Bicycling Golf	Motocross Golf
Political views	Democrat	Agnostic (Really. I am a registered Independent!)
Education	Bucknell University, BA, Human Resource Management; Johns Hopkins, MA, Marketing	American University, BSBA
Faith	We belong to a contemporary Christian church where we enjoy the band that leads us and the relevant message we hear each week.	

Interests we share	Traveling (domestically or abroad — we travel very well together), entertaining our friends in our home, our kids' activities (yes, we are coaches and taxi drivers and scout leaders). We really love to go to dueling piano bars, and always try to find one in any new city we visit (we'll be the ones singing badly but enthusiastically).	
Personal interests	As a "jack of all trades, master of none" I like a lot of different things, and am up for trying just about anything anyone invites me to. I enjoy following sports, comedy clubs, theatre, fitness, my kids' sports, my faith, dining out, movies, traveling with my wife, skiing, reading.	I grew up in a family with a lot of guys, and tagged along on a lot of their adventures, so perhaps that shaped my preferences. I like skiing, watching sports, comedy clubs, theatre, yoga, my faith, dining out, movies, spa treatments, shopping, acting (though I don't get much of a chance these days).

#2 — We'll give you a little primer on the *tone* of this book. We are married and happy, and we write from this place. But we are also *normal* people who have work stuff and family crap and baggage and everything that goes along with *real life*.

We hope this book is sometimes witty, always honest, and often even sarcastic. So if you find yourself struggling to decipher a certain chapter, we suggest you channel your inner Jon Stewart and then hopefully things should make sense!

#3 — We'll give you some answers to questions your friends might ask if they see this book in your bag or hanging out on your kitchen table. Questions like… "Who are these people anyway?"

Answer: We are college-educated professionals who have spent time thinking about these things and talking to those who have been successful in their relationships. We are NOT counselors or therapists. But we know that sometimes it is helpful to get straight answers from people who have been there and done that. And that is who we are — people who have weathered the storms of our relationship and want to share what we have learned with you (in a fun and honest way).

Or…"Why do we need to spend the time and money to go away for a weekend?"

Answer: This is really an investment in your future, and one that can pay dividends *much* greater than those same dollars stashed in your bank account (but then again, that's not saying much lately). Because something magical happens when you take time and energy out of your hectic lives and devote it to making your union stronger. At the end of your retreat you will feel reenergized and refocused and reconnected with your partner. And then you will be able to conquer the world! And *that* is certainly worth a modest investment.

Or..."Can't we just tackle these things at home over the course of a few evenings?"

Answer: Sure, you could take time each night over the next several weeks and address one topic each night. But will you?!? We're guessing NOT. You'll get distracted, you'll lose focus, and other priorities will emerge (like the all-important finale of *The Bachelor*). And that is why a retreat is important. Because it allows you to get away from all the distractions and really focus on yourselves and your issues. Besides...if you get away, you get to build in *fun* and *relaxation;* two things you are very unlikely to get on a Tuesday night after a long day at the office.

So there you have it — some background, insight, and answers. All that is left is for you to dive in and have your own 48 Hour Retreat.

We are very sure you are smart enough to find your way to the transformation of your relationship on your own with some dedicated time and attention. You picked up this book, right? And we think that makes you brilliant!

OUR STORY: This is the Early Warning System

That's right. We wanted to warn you right up front. In these boxes you will find our personal stories. If you are digging our vibe you can dive right in, but if you are getting too much of our autobiographies you can skip over them. Your choice! Of course we're not going to tell you stories about how much laundry we have to do or what we had for dinner last night. We'll tell you little bits and pieces about our retreat experiences over the years. Sometimes they might make you laugh; sometimes they might make you scratch your head. Overall we hope you'll get the point that we've been there too...and we are better for it!

HOW WE'VE ORGANIZED THIS BOOK

(Whatcha Got There?)

HOW WE'VE ORGANIZED THIS BOOK
(Whatcha Got There?)

Before you get too far along, we wanted to give you the rough outline of your journey. We've divided this book into four sections, and each of these sections is very different.

- **SECTION 1 — MAKING THE CASE —** Understanding why this 48 Hour Retreat can help you and what you can expect to accomplish.

- **SECTION 2 — PREPARING FOR YOUR RETREAT —** The advance planning necessary to make sure your retreat is a success.

- **THE INTERMISSION —** It is exactly that … a little break in the action.

- **SECTION 3 — THE WORKBOOK —** The "doing it" part of the book with ten of your most likely retreat topics explained in depth with suggested items to cover, questions to ask, and THE METHOD to work through them.

- **SECTION 4 — MAKING IT STICK —** The final section is about what you should do after your retreat is over to continue all your good progress.

- **BONUS — THE WEBSITE** (www. 48HourRetreat.com) — Our website that has a ton of extra resources for you (some free since you bought this book, others for a nominal fee). Some things you can find there:

  - Books and other websites that may be resources for your retreat

  - Worksheets to support the materials in the workbook section

  - Our blog

  - Tips and tricks from others who have already done a retreat

Sounds pretty straightforward and well-organized, if we do say so ourselves!

Fun Fact: The chapter titles are an example of how compromise works in our relationship. Richard wanted the titles to be clear and concise so you know what is coming. Amanda likes things more creative and fun. So voilà—we have a title that says what it is, and a subtitle that adds a bit of flare to each chapter.

SECTION 1
Making the Case

CHAPTER 1
HOW THIS STARTED
(Let's Start at the Very Beginning/
It's a Very Good Place to Start)

CHAPTER 1
HOW THIS STARTED
(Let's Start at the Very Beginning/
It's a Very Good Place to Start)

"The unexamined life is not worth living."
— Socrates

OUR STORY: The Inaugural Event

Here's how our initial retreat conversation went way back in 1996:

Richard: "Let's spend a weekend away together planning for our future. Sort of like a corporate retreat. It'll be great!"

Amanda: "What?!?"

Richard: "Yeah, we'll spend the weekend talking about our values, goals, plans, budgets, and more."

Amanda: "Are you kidding me?"

Richard: "Really! Trust me!"

Amanda: "Really???"

Richard: "We'll go to a hotel for the weekend."

Amanda: "Hold on, I'll pack my bags!"

The 48 Hour Relationship Retreat is based on a do-it-yourself retreat system we developed and have been using since 1996. It's been truly transformational in our lives and we know it can be the same for you!

Originally Richard, the one with the management background and an unnatural addiction to business books, thought that if successful companies could benefit from getting together annually to reflect and plan, we could too.

Richard has always been big into goal-setting and planning and was immersed in the Franklin Day Planner system, so talking about our future seemed, to him, the most natural thing for two people starting a life together to do.

But Amanda wasn't so sure. Introspection and long-range planning weren't really her thing. She was more of a "face life as it comes at you" kind of a person. However, because she was "goofy in love" (and because it involved a weekend away at a hotel), Amanda agreed to the first retreat.

WHAT HAPPENED AFTER THAT

What started out as Richard's idea eventually became the "can't-miss event" of our year, and we've managed to hold a retreat annually since — well, except for the one year we missed, and that year was B-A-D!

Over the years we've found our annual retreat to be an amazing way to connect, assess our relationship, and make the changes we see as necessary to be able to reach our dreams TOGETHER. It's made a very positive impact on our marriage and we feel it can help any long-term relationship, married or not.

Throughout the past couple of decades, we've expanded and tweaked our agenda, but the basic core has remained the same — get away, have fun, make positive changes in our lives, and proactively plan for the future. And we've always wanted to do it within our own parameters — without getting all touchy-feely and sharing our "issues" with other people.

When it comes right down to it, we feel *we* are the experts on *our* relationship. We know what *our* struggles are and we know what has worked for *us* in the past to fix *our* problems. And we believe the same is true of you, too!

You are the experts on *your* relationship. Sure, there are professionals who can ask you questions and guide you to uncover your answers (in fact, that is sort of what this book is about), but we don't think you need to spend endless hours on a therapist's couch to make progress. In the end, *you* know more about *your* circumstances, *your* goals, and *your* dreams than anyone else.

RICHARD SPEAKS

(Let me explain myself, men of America, because maybe once I do you'll see where I'm going with this.)

I know this is going to sound so "guy" of me, but it really wasn't an emotional thing when I came up with the idea of The Retreat. I mean, I was in love, but it was really more of a practical business move when it started out.

My thinking came from the business world in which I'd been to several corporate gatherings where we talked and discussed and plotted and schemed for the future. It seemed to make sense that we would take that same approach and apply it to our marriage. We're a team, a corporation of two; so why wouldn't we get together and discuss the bigger issues?

THE CORPORATE PERSPECTIVE

Each year, virtually every business and organization of any size meets to review the past year. It seems obvious that taking some time to look back and see what went well and what went poorly is a good thing for organizations to do for many reasons:

1. Learning from mistakes
2. Celebrating successes
3. Determining which goals were missed and why

It also seems obvious that a business should put together some sort of plan for the coming months and/or years. And, of course, most do. The purposes of annual planning are many, including:

1. Determining how to allocate scarce resources
2. Understanding potential and actual threats
3. Identifying opportunities for growth

With demands on employees and the distractions of the workplace, most organizations choose to pull key employees together to evaluate and make decisions in a group setting. For some companies, a multi-hour meeting in a conference room works best. For others, a trip to a more remote location like a wilderness lodge without cell reception serves as the best way to help everyone focus on the task at hand.

Whether it's a brief meeting or an elaborate off-site retreat, there are a few key elements that are common to almost all organizations:

1. Evaluating the past is a *regular, formal* process.
2. Planning for the future is a *regular, formal* process.
3. The evaluating and planning processes are done as a *team*.
4. It's helpful if these processes are done in a location that *minimizes distractions*.

In today's world of 24-hour-a-day access, finding time away to really focus is critical.

By now you've probably figured out where we're going with this. (Hint: We're suggesting your relationship is analogous to a corporation — at least for planning purposes!)

"SO WHAT'S THIS GOT TO DO WITH US?" YOU ASK.

Really, if you think about it, the same rules can easily apply to a relationship as well. In fact, we'd argue that applying what most business organizations already know can be transformative in your lives, too.

Too often we hear that couples get caught up in the everyday craziness and they don't take some time to make plans. Both people are running at high speed but they aren't working together *toward the same goals* and they aren't spending the time they should on the things that they value the most! (We take retreats, and we still fall victim to this problem, so we know it's happening to you, too!!!)

If you don't believe us, just answer these questions:

- Are you doing the things that are the top priorities in your relationship?
- Are you saving for the things that you've both agreed are the most important?
- Do you invest the time you want on the things that really matter?
- Are you both working together for the same goals?
- Do you really know what is important to each other?

Taking 48 hours out of your year to stop the merry-go-round that is life and reconnect with your partner can be magical. Also spending time to identify dreams, goals, and priorities, and then developing a plan to actually reach them, is amazingly powerful stuff. Knowing that you and your partner have a plan for the future, and then working on that plan together, can literally change your life in a dramatic way. Does that sound a little overblown? Perhaps. But after you take your retreat you will be using these same superlatives!

If you give it 48 hours, we know you'll emerge refreshed, refocused, and inspired. And a stronger couple.

What two people in a committed relationship can accomplish when they're working together is inspiring. But you need to stop the madness of daily life, sit down, and actually talk about it first! You need to be proactive — not reactive!

(We really think we should be charging you $20,000.00 for this book given the incredible benefits you'll get, but our publisher gently suggested that that price tag might turn away a few prospective buyers!)

OUR STORY: Holy Snow, Batman!

Our first retreat (the one that Amanda originally dreaded) ended up being a very fun and funny weekend. We got stranded at the Holiday Inn in Washington, DC, by the crazy blizzard of January 1996. We walked several miles in the middle of snow-covered roads to get to the only restaurant that we could find open. (Thank goodness they had wings and beer.)

The good news was that we didn't have to pay for the extra hotel night. And when we left, we were very pleased that our car had been in the garage all weekend and we didn't have to spend hours shoveling it out of a plow-induced snow bank.

The unintended consequence of the blizzard was that we had extra time to work through all of our wedding plans and make *important* life decisions (like live band or DJ). We think it was divine intervention. Maybe the extra time was what we needed to make the weekend special — it certainly made it memorable. And because it was such a great weekend, we did it again the next year (Amanda still wasn't completely sold, but she was certainly more open to it that year) and then the next year and so on, and so on, and so on!

CHAPTER 2
ANSWERING THE CRITICS

(Okay, Doubting Thomas – Bring It ON!)

CHAPTER 2
ANSWERING THE CRITICS
(Okay, Doubting Thomas —
Bring It ON!)

"Obstacles are those frightful things you see when you take your eyes off your goal."
— Henry Ford
"A goal is a dream with a deadline."
— Napoleon Hill

OUR STORY: What We've Gained from Our Retreats

So many times it seems that our careers or our kids are taking over our lives. We come home tired and it's not a good time to talk, there's always something going on, and we're exhausted. Our relationship becomes the last thing we really worry about.

But for us, this retreat is truly about setting the stones for our foundation. We still have those times of disconnection, but the great thing is that we have learned how to identify them because we know what it looks like to be connected. For us, when we are disconnected we don't completely panic because we say, "Okay, we know what it looks like to be connected, and we've dealt with this. Here are the five things that we need to accomplish to get back on track. It's been a long time since we had date night. When we have date night it is always better. Let's do that."

We have a plan. We're not perfect. We don't practice what we preach all the time. But when we're not practicing it at least we know what we should be doing and we can get back to it more easily.

When we were contemplating writing this book, several caring friends who were playing devil's advocates asked us some very good (and tough) questions. We thought you might have these same questions, too, so we decided to just address them head-on here.

YOU MIGHT BE THINKING THIS, TOO

Why do we need goals and planning?

Richard has always loved a quote from an unknown author who observed that "Some people make things happen, some watch things happen, and some wonder what happened." A retreat is a time to be proactive — to examine your situation, reassess your goals, and make plans to achieve your dreams.

In *The 48 Hour Relationship Retreat*, our goal is to identify and work on basically two areas:

1. Things in our current lives and relationship that we would like to change or enhance.

2. Key personal and family dreams that we would like to accomplish in the future.

Then we create action plans so that we don't just hope for the future but are proactively moving forward toward what's important to us. That's it. It's really that simple!

Most of us lead fairly unexamined lives. We are so busy working to pay the bills, running our kids from one place to the next, and hanging out with friends and family that we don't take time to actually think about our lives and make a plan for success. Getting through tomorrow is as far ahead as many of us can think sometimes (us included).

However, if we don't get clear on our goals and dreams, we then end up just plodding along from day to day instead of creating our lives the way we want them to be. Do we really want to look up one day and realize we never fulfilled our dreams and never really knew our partner and our children in the best possible ways?

If you talk to people who experience empty nest syndrome, many will tell you that they feel alone and sad because they don't have a purpose and they feel disconnected from their partner. They were so "heads down" for years, working and raising their family, that they didn't take time to plan for their own future. Don't let this be you!

There is so much to do that we wouldn't even know where to start.

Because we know that you have tons to do in your regular life, we don't want this process to be a big burden. We've made it extra easy and simple so you can use every minute of your retreat wisely and well. (Oh yeah, we want you to be able to grab some rest, relaxation, and fun at the same time, too.)

It's a common observation that most people spend more time planning for their vacations than planning for their retirement or for their careers or for their kids' education. If you really think about it, you, too, would probably have to admit that you aren't spending as much time as you should discussing and planning for the important things in your relationship. (Okay, we agree; vacation planning IS much more fun!)

So do something about that imbalance!!!

This just sounds like a recipe for a weekend of arguments.

This would be a crummy book if we were setting you up for that, wouldn't it?!? Really, no worries; *The 48 Hour Relationship Retreat* will guide you through the process step by step. This is your handbook for *your own retreat*. It gives you an easy-to-execute model that will have you accomplishing victories along the way, and those small victories will encourage you to dream big and plan to succeed.

Why do we need 48 hours?

This retreat is designed to be held over a weekend. Ideally you and your partner would devote two full days (48 hours) to your retreat. We have found that this amount of time allows you to really delve into the details at the heart of your issues. It also allows for ample time to enjoy yourselves. Remember — FUN! If you cannot take an entire weekend, you can visit the website for shortened agendas for a one- or one-and-a-half-day retreat. But especially for your first time out, we strongly encourage you to jump into the deep end...take the BIG PLUNGE and fully commit. What's the worst thing that could happen? You'd come back rested and relaxed with BIG DREAMS and the plans to make them happen?!?

Or here is another answer:

Because less time is not enough and more time really isn't practical. We have tested the agendas in this book over the years and we have found that a full weekend is necessary in order to give each subject the time and attention it needs. And yet, if you spend more than a weekend on a retreat, you are likely to get distracted and not get to the point.

> This chapter was going on a bit with nothing to break it up, so we thought we would put a box in here. That is all. Please move along now.

Are these people who wrote this book actually qualified?

We're not marriage therapists, but we *can* provide you with a compilation of methods and tools that have been life tested by "normal" people.

- We are a fairly representative couple of achievers who enjoy being proactive in life.

- We are more sarcastic (and perhaps funnier) than your average therapist.

- We know what worked for us.

- We know that *you* are the experts on *your* relationship.

- You don't have to come and sit on our couch (we're almost never home, so it really would just be creepy to come in and find you on our sofa).

- We can show you how to hash it out between yourselves with no one watching.

- You won't be judged on the bad crying faces you make.

- We can vouch for the fact that a 48 Hour Retreat is like months of therapy rolled into one weekend. (Think about how many weekly sessions you would have to go through to make progress on all of these issues with a therapist.)

- This retreat won't make you work on issues you don't have.

- Look at all the money you'll save!

Tell us again...why do we need to do a retreat?

Basically we answered this in Chapter 1, but we'll give you another answer here.

Our friends who know that we take this retreat every year often marvel at it. They are curious and ask us questions: "What do you do?" "Does it really work?" "What happens when it's over?" But the biggest question they *never* really ask is... *Why?* That is the most important question!

We do a retreat because, like corporations, churches, small businesses, and other organizations, it ensures that we take time out of the craziness of our everyday lives to focus on the important things and the big picture. We've found that having fun, working on our challenges, and dreaming together are the stones that form the foundation of our relationship and our family. We make sure our canoe is headed in the right direction and that we know who's paddling on which side.

Amanda's mother often says that the best gift anyone can ever give to their children is a strong marriage. And she is a VERY wise woman. (She's also going to read this, so we get major points for saying that.) We take time each year to get it right — to work through the unpleasant parts to make the rest of the year worth it, to make our lives work out the way we want them to, and to create the kind of relationship that supports each of us and our children.

Couples grow out of their relationships because they aren't working on them together. The retreat is an opportunity to really connect, to head off in the same direction together, to take the time to understand each other, set goals, and make plans together. After each of our retreats we leave feeling reenergized. We come up with exciting lists, draw up plans, have great goals, operate like a team, and we know we can get a lot done because we have each other's backs.

You can do this, too!

AND HERE ARE A FEW MORE POSITIVE THOUGHTS FROM US:

- We believe in a bigger vision for you than you do right now (but you will soon see it for yourself).

- We believe that every family has the potential to be a GREAT family.

- We know that if you are both working with the same goals in mind, you are much more likely to achieve them than if you were working at cross purposes.

- Honesty, while scary, actually increases your intimacy factor.

- After your retreat you'll be able to tackle projects you've only dreamed of.

- Children thrive in a happy home.

- Most important, we believe you can do it!

NOW THAT WE'VE CONVINCED YOU, DON'T JUST SIT THERE — DO SOMETHING!

This book is not meant to provide a passive experience. It is not a bedside reading book to help you get to sleep at night. This is an active book meant to guide you through a weekend relationship experience to enhance what you already have together.

There are exercises to do, discussions to have, and plans to be made. If you make it to the workbook section (beginning with Chapter 8) and are just reading, not making arrangements, then put this book down. Or better yet, get off your butts and get on the phone to your travel agent.

Take the time — it's just one weekend — and you won't regret it. A friend recently asked, "You plan out the next year of your life in just 48 hours?" And we said resoundingly, "YES!"

And with *The 48 Hour Relationship Retreat,* you can do it, too!

YOU'RE IN, RIGHT?!

Do you believe you can do it? Are you tired of all the "rah rah" PMA (positive mental attitude) stuff and just want to get on with it? Then read on...because as The Carpenters sang, "We've only just begun..."

Richard: "We're going to quote a Carpenters song here?"

Amanda: "Yep."

Richard: "Really?"

Amanda: "Yep."

Richard: "Right here in the middle of our super serious book?"

Amanda: "Yep."

Richard: "Sounds super-de-duper!"

DISCLAIMER:

We are not certified counselors, couples therapists, or members of the clergy. (We own a couch, but the only time anyone lies on it is when someone is sick or there is a game on.) Use of *The 48 Hour Relationship Retreat* can cause such common side effects as unstoppable diarrhea, dry heaves, scurvy, temporary blindness, and convulsions leading to a coma. Rarely, with prolonged use, other side effects can occur such as limited bladder control, festering boils, or an erection lasting more than four hours. Okay, we have never experienced any of that on our retreats, but we thought we would cover all of our bases. *The 48 Hour Relationship Retreat* is intended to share our retreat experiences. The information provided is open to personal interpretation and is not intended to diagnose, cure, or prevent any disease or other medical or psychological condition. If there is a section that doesn't work for you—scrap it! If you need to add a section that's missing, do it. (And then visit our site to tell us where we missed the boat for your unique situation.)

SECTION 2
Preparing For Your Retreat

CHAPTER 3
TIME AND PLACE
(Hi Ho, Hi Ho! It's Off to Work You Go!)

CHAPTER 3
TIME AND PLACE
(Hi Ho, Hi Ho! It's Off to Work You Go!)

"It is thrifty to prepare today for the wants of tomorrow."
— Aesop, *The Ant and the Grasshopper*

In order to have a fun and rewarding retreat, you need to do a little legwork in advance of your trip. Notice that the first thing mentioned was fun. In today's world of work followed by the gym followed by carpool followed by volunteer assignments, there is often little time left for fun and relaxation. While this weekend is aimed at enriching your relationship, you should also have some time dedicated to enjoying yourself. If done correctly, you can use your retreat not only to map out your future but also to rejuvenate your soul.

With that in mind, this chapter outlines the steps necessary to assure that you:

1. Have all the information you need with you

2. Are well-prepared for your retreat

3. Are focused on yourself and your relationship and not on the logistics of your retreat

Do this work in advance of your retreat (at least a couple of weeks), and you will reap the benefits of a well-organized and successful get-away.

SELECT A DATE

- Find a weekend clear of conflicts.

- The beginning of the year is opportune, but not necessary. Don't let it hinder you!

- Do not schedule your retreat with a big project or other stress-inducing event coming right after the retreat.

So look at your calendar now — YES, RIGHT NOW — and commit to that weekend. Write it in pen today!

> **TIP:** Please resist the temptation to break this retreat up into its components and spread it out over several weeks. When you devote a weekend to this exercise, your thoughts, dreams, and inspirations can build upon one another. We have also found that if you try to do one section a night over several weeks, you'll give up when the going gets tough and not get to the heart of the matter.

SELECT A LOCATION

As soon as you have your date you should consider your location. As with any regular vacation, some destinations book up months in advance, while at others you can walk right up to the front desk and get a room. So then the question becomes, what tickles your fancy?

Does the beach float your boat? Do the mountains peak your curiosity (yes, pun intended)? Is one of you attracted to the hustle and bustle of the city while the other would rather hibernate in a ski chalet? Pick a location for your retreat that will nourish your souls and make you feel comfortable. Remember, try to find a location that has benefits for both of you. For example, a downtown hotel that is just a short drive to great hiking trails might be just right to balance both your desires.

> **TIP:** Find a place that fits your budget and your personality. Fuming over a bad location all weekend will distract from your purpose and goals.

If you are on a budget, you don't need to go to some exotic location for the weekend and spend hundreds of dollars. This format is made to fit any location, any time. If you don't have the money to get away, you can stay at home (and send the kids out) and have your retreat there.

Remember that no matter where you go, vacation is not your *first* priority; your retreat is. If there is something special you would like to do at the hotel or in the area, make a note of it and use it as a relaxation break. Just make sure you schedule it into your weekend so it doesn't take away from your main goal — your relationship.

Some Alternatives to a Hotel

Here are some creative alternatives to a traditional hotel (and some considerations that come along with them):

Camping or other *au naturel* locations — Often a very cost-effective alternative, but just a few things to keep in mind: Food — make sure you have enough of it. Electricity — the lack of electricity will affect your ability to use a computer and the number of daylight hours available to have discussions. Take these things into account when you are planning your agenda and your supplies.

Bed & Breakfast (B&B) — Often romantic with fireplaces and four-poster beds, B&Bs can provide a getaway with a homey touch. One consideration about B&Bs is that the common space of the house can sometimes be quite busy, leaving you only your room in which to work.

House Swap — If you have kids, it might be easier for them to stay in their own environment. In this case, consider a house swap. Talk to the babysitter (friend, grandparents, etc.) and see if they will come to your house while you stay in their home. Since it isn't your house, it is almost like being at a B&B...you won't be distracted by the emails you need to write, weeds you need to pull, or projects on your "honey do" list.

ARRANGE FOR THE SITTER

If your children are young (or maybe they are four-footed), make arrangements for daycare. Here are several options that might work for you and allow you to enjoy your time away:

- **Ask a family member.** This would be a great time for grandparents, aunts, or uncles to spend some quality time with the youngins.

- **Ask a neighbor.** If your children are old enough to stay at home but you still feel a little uneasy, ask a neighbor to check in from time to time.

- **Ask a daycare provider.** If your child is in daycare, often the daycare workers are happy to pick up extra money on the weekends.

- **Ask your friends.** Who doesn't need a break? Your friends with children may be happy to watch your children in exchange for their own kid-free weekend in the future. (You might even suggest they go on a retreat themselves.)

FOR YOUR COMFORT

No matter where you are, there are a few things that are necessary for a successful retreat:

1. **A comfortable place to talk** — Sometimes it's nice to sit on the floor or laze on the couch; other times a good writing surface is necessary.

2. **No television** — Make the commitment to turn off the TV for the whole weekend (except maybe during your break times). Television is a passive activity and does not allow you and your partner to interact.

3. **Music** can add to the mood.

4. **Turn off all wireless devices** — cell, iPad, etc. Tell your friends, family, and workplace that you are going on your retreat for the weekend and will be unreachable.

5. **Food** — Make sure you have enough snacks for the weekend. You don't want to interrupt an important discussion because your tummy is grumbly. (Richard can get *very* unfocused when hungry, so we've learned from experience.)

OUR STORY: Meet Me at the Ritz

We have tried doing a retreat both ways—at a hotel, and at home. We have to tell you that while our retreat at home was better than not having a retreat at all, staying at home just wasn't nearly as good as the years when we went away. It didn't feel as special, and we were often distracted (the dog needed to go out or the pile of dirty laundry was calling from the corner of the room). And we tried; trust us. We even went to our local Panera for lunch and thought we would discuss a topic over our soup and sandwiches. The problem: one of our friendly neighbors spied us at our table, came over to chat, and before we knew it we had run through thirty minutes of valuable retreat time.

So now we know. Our retreat is so important to us that we make it a top priority each year, budget accordingly, and we get away (usually only within driving distance so we don't waste all of our time on planes, trains, and automobiles).

CHAPTER 4
THE AGENDA
(Design on a Dime)

CHAPTER 4
THE AGENDA
(Design on a Dime)

"Make no little plans; they have no magic to stir men's blood."
— Daniel Hudson Burnham

DESIGN *YOUR* AGENDA

Now that you have committed to a date and made your reservations, it is time to create an agenda for *your* retreat that is going to suit *your* needs. You will need about two hours to devote to the process of developing your agenda, and you need to do it *together*. This advance work is the foundation of your retreat and it will pay off if you spend the time now. So grab this book and a glass of wine and spend an evening together (or a cup of coffee on a Saturday morning). Make it a nice experience rather than a chore. Have fun with it, poke fun at yourselves for your foibles, and get excited about the possibilities.

Select Topics

Sit down with your partner and take a good look at each of the workbook chapters in the second half of this book and the discussion points one by one. Make an assessment of each point as to its importance in *your* relationship. As different as people are, their issues are equally different. This book tries to include the major topics that most individuals and couples struggle with, but your personal struggles may be different.

Make changes or additions to the agenda that you feel are necessary to reflect the issues you are dealing with right now. Add points under each chapter that you think are important to discuss. Don't shy away from the tough issues, though — that is the point of your retreat: working on the stuff of everyday to make plans to accomplish your dreams. Also, if one person thinks a section is worthy of inclusion, then it is worthy of inclusion. Remember, the goal here is to meet the needs of both of you and make the relationship stronger as a result.

A few sample agendas have been included at the end of this chapter. The agenda items are put in a specific order to allow for a flow of conversation. Some sections should come before others because they build upon one another, and yet others are placed where they are to provide a break (i.e., "lighter" topics interspersed between "heavier" topics). The order, of course, is based on the topics that are easier and more difficult in *our* relationship. For you it may be much different.

Allot Time

Once you have decided on the topics to be included, then decide on the amount of time you are going to devote to each issue. You can use the times listed on the sample agendas as guidelines for your planning. The time at your retreat will fly by, so we encourage you to try to be thoughtful. You may want to use your driving time to discuss issues, or maybe a lighter topic can be covered over dinner.

And don't forget to schedule in the FUN (as Amanda likes to remind). Remember that there is more to your retreat than just work; it is about re-energizing your batteries and achieving balance. So find some balance in your weekend and make room for some time having fun together and maybe even some individual time as well — massage, driving range, nice long bath, jogging?

TIPS FOR CREATING *YOUR* AGENDA:

Goals and Values should be placed fairly early in your retreat. Getting clarity about these (and understanding your partner's viewpoint) helps you make decisions in the other areas of your retreat.

Relationship is a section in which you can work on communication and basic relationship issues. Doing some of this work early in your retreat gives you tools to use in the rest of your retreat. Sort of a "practice what we preach" concept.

Spirituality is usually scheduled for Sunday morning since that is a time often devoted to religious services. If your services are held at another time, you may want to move this section to the time that you usually devote to the practice of your faith.

Finances can be a contentious issue for a lot of couples. (It used to bring Amanda to tears.) If this is the case in your relationship, you might want to address this issue early on so you don't have the "big axe" hanging over your head. We have also included a budget *review* section that should take place at the end of your retreat. This allows you to revisit your budget based on priorities and goals that may have changed as a result of your discussions.

Intimacy is often scheduled for later in the evening. If this type of discussion is a hard one for you, we suggest taking a bath or having the discussion over a candlelight dinner. We also recommend this time so that you can put into practice what you discuss.

For us, the lighter topics tend to be **Health and Fitness, Family, Home,** and **Scheduling**. We intersperse these with other topics to provide discussions that aren't as contentious or demanding. Again, for you some of these issues may actually be the hot spots in your relationship and should be moved around.

If we haven't said this enough, this is *your* retreat, so adjust accordingly.

MAKE YOUR HOMEWORK ASSIGNMENTS

DISCLAIMER (yes, another disclaimer):

When we say homework, we're not talking about pulling an all-nighter here. Most of what we suggest is a little pre-thinking for each chapter. Really, don't dread this. Relax!

An agenda is great, but the pre-work doesn't stop there. Without doing a little bit of reading, you are going to spend some of your valuable retreat time just figuring out what you're supposed to be talking about rather than getting to the heart of the matter. Divvy up the responsibilities for each agenda item between the two of you. So one person doesn't feel too burdened (and to show a commitment by both parties), each person should take responsibility for leading an equal amount of the agenda items.

Much like a class or a meeting, there needs to be one person who begins the conversation on each topic. If you divide the responsibility, then one person will not seem to be confrontational or appear to be bossy. If one of you does not feel comfortable in this leadership role, we encourage you to use this division of labor: alternating who starts the next item. It will give some sense of balance to your retreat and allow you to exercise leadership skills that every person should develop. (And if one person has a problem sharing leadership in the relationship, this is probably an agenda item you should add to your retreat.)

When you skim your chapters (for which you have been assigned responsibility), take note of homework that might go along with each chapter. Is there thinking that should be done in advance? Do you need to find information from various websites? Make assignments for one or both of the partners to complete prior to leaving for your retreat. These assignments may or may not go along with the responsibilities you just identified. Say Amanda is going to run the finances section, but Richard is better at playing with spreadsheets...it is okay for Richard to crunch the numbers, and it might just make sense.

Whatever the assignments are, make sure that you feel the division of labor is fair. That does not mean that it has to be fifty-fifty, just that you each feel you are contributing to the whole given your current commitments.

> **TIP:** Gather your supplies in advance of your retreat. You will want to have the correct support materials on hand. In advance of your retreat, take the time to go to the library or bookstore, or search the web and find the materials you require. A resource list is included on our website — www.48HourRetreat.com.

SAMPLE RETREAT AGENDAS

We've provided two sample two-day agendas based on how we typically organize our agenda. They reflect the amounts of time we have found are most helpful to both accomplish all we want to get done, and yet to have a relaxing weekend and work in some fun as well. You have two options; either use one of our pre-made agendas for your retreat, or create an agenda of your own. You can visit our website to find some sample agendas for shorter retreats (not that we recommend it, but we know some of you are going to do it anyway — do we sound like your parents here?).

SAMPLE AGENDA #1 — THE TYPE A'S RETREAT

(This is a sample. Repeat, this is ONLY a sample. Remember, you get to make up your own!)

FRIDAY

Time	Subject	Book Chapter
2-2:30pm	Beginning the Retreat	Chapter 10
2:30-2:45pm	*Break*	
2:45-3:45pm	Goals & Values	Chapter 11
3:45-4pm	*Break*	
4-5pm	Finances	Chapter 13
5-5:15pm	*Break*	
5:15-6pm	Health & Wellness	Chapter 16
6-6:15pm	*Break*	
6:15-7pm	Intimacy	Chapter 20
7-9pm	*Shower, Dinner, etc.*	
9pm-?	Practice, Practice, Practice	

TIP: Intersperse your difficult subjects with easier subjects or breaks. If you know you have one topic that is sure to ignite controversy and difficult feelings, plan to tackle that subject and then schedule yourselves for some time apart. Maybe you'll talk about your family and then one of you can go for a walk and the other person takes a nap. This separation allows you to have a cooling-off period.

SATURDAY

Time	Subject	Book Chapter
9-10am	Careers	Chapter 14
10-10:15am	*Break*	
10:15-11:30am	Family	Chapter 18
11:30-11:45am	*Break*	
11:45am-12:30pm	Home	Chapter 17
12:30-1:30pm	*Lunch*	
1:30-3:30pm	Relationship	Chapter 12
3:30-4pm	*Break*	
4-5pm	Scheduling	Chapter 19
5-6pm	Your Topic Here	Chapter 21
6pm-?	Relaxation & Entertainment	

SUNDAY

Time	Subject	Book Chapter
9-10am	Spirituality	Chapter 15
10-10:15am	*Break*	
10:15-11am	Budget Review	Chapter 22
11am-12noon	Making Plans	Chapter 23
12noon-2pm	*Lunch*	
2pm	Depart for Home (reenergized and refocused)	

RETREAT SAMPLE #2 — THE RELAXED RETREAT

(Again, just a sample agenda people — tweak as you please!)

FRIDAY

Time	Subject	Book Chapter
2-2:30pm	Beginning the Retreat	Chapter 10
2:30-3:30pm	Goals & Values	Chapter 11
3:30-3:45pm	*Break*	
3:45-5:00pm	Relationship	Chapter 12
5-5:30pm	*Break*	
5:30-6:15pm	Intimacy	Chapter 20
6:15-7pm	Shower, etc.	
7-9pm	*Dinner*	
9pm-?	Practice, Practice, Practice	

SATURDAY

Time	Subject	Book Chapter
10-11am	Finances	Chapter 13
11-11:15am	*Break*	
11:15am-12noon	Home	Chapter 17
12noon-12:30pm	*Break*	
12:30-1:30pm	Family	Chapter 18
1:30-3:15pm	*Lunch, Leisure Time*	
3:15-4pm	Scheduling	Chapter 19
4-5pm	Careers	Chapter 14
5-7pm	Leisure Time	
7-9pm	*Dinner*	
9pm-?	Evening Entertainment	

SUNDAY

Time	Subject	Book Chapter
10-10:30am	Health & Wellness	Chapter 16
10:30-11am	Spirituality	Chapter 15
11am-12noon	Budget Review	Chapter 22
12noon-1pm	*Lunch*	
1-2pm	Making Plans	Chapter 23
2pm	Depart for Home (reenergized and refocused	

So what are you waiting for?!? Make your own agenda now!

And when you're done, celebrate. You might even feel closer to each other just by going through this first step. Take some time and enjoy the good feelings. If this first phase was challenging, don't be discouraged. It just means that you have some important work to do at your retreat. But the good news is that the greater the obstacles, the more accomplished you will feel when you overcome them!

CHAPTER 5
GROUND RULES
(Leveling the Playing Field)

CHAPTER 5
GROUND RULES
(Leveling the Playing Field)

"It is hard to believe that a man is telling the truth when you know that you would lie if you were in his place."
— Henry Louis Mencken, *A Little Book in C Major*, 1916

When we told Amanda's brilliant friend Barb about our retreats and our thoughts of turning our idea into a book, she raised a good question: "But how do you discuss difficult topics without getting all pissed at each other and blowing the whole weekend?"

The answer to this question might just be the key to your success this weekend. Honesty, criticism, and trying to agree on plans are difficult and emotional issues. Working through them is challenging and can bring up anger, frustration, and even tears. We know. We've been there, too. Oh yeah, we've had tears and tough discussions even though we like to pretend we're perfect!!

But with experience we have found that you don't need to dread this. You just need a few tools to help you change your model of behavior and a few ground rules to help guide you through the weekend.

This topic got its own chapter for three reasons:

1. Ground rules are important so that everyone is playing on the same field.

2. Each of you may want to refer back to these pages at one point or another, so we wanted to make it easy to find.

3. As we mentioned in the introduction, we love sports, and they all have rules!

Of course these are *our* ground rules and *you* can add any others you feel necessary, but this is a good place to start.

TWELVE BRILLIANT GROUND RULES BY WHICH TO RUN YOUR RETREAT

1. Have fun — Hmmmmm…have you heard this somewhere before? That's because it is central to the success of your retreat. Which would you rather do: spend a relaxing and engaging weekend with your partner, or spend a weekend having heated and difficult conversations? That's a no-brainer! So put this in the right perspective. This weekend is about having a good time while you work on issues that will help you and your partner reconnect and create a plan to reach your dreams.

2. *Everyone* does *all* the work — No one can take a pass and say, "I'll do it later." You have an entire weekend, so use the time to do the work NOW. It is only natural to want to ignore a section that is uncomfortable in favor of subjects you like better. Fight against your inner demons! If everyone digs through the tough stuff, the rewards will be much greater. And if you slack off, you are only cheating yourself.

3. Listen — Really listen to what your partner is saying. Practice active listening — resist the temptation to jump in and finish his or her sentence or refute a statement. After you are done talking, let your partner summarize what they heard you say to make sure that you were understood.

4. Be honest — The goal is to get to the real heart of matters in your relationship. Though it may be uncomfortable, try to look deeply into yourself and find the real roots of your feelings. Share these with your partner. Also try to hear what your partner is really saying, not what you are projecting onto them. You should be honest about how you feel. Don't say what you *think* your partner wants to hear. Say what *you really feel.* This honesty is the key to understanding why you behave in certain ways and why you make certain decisions. When your partner truly understands the *why* behind your actions, they better understand you. But again, say it gently and lovingly.

5. Be accepting — If your partner is being honest (as we just said they should be), accept what they have said as the truth about how they feel. Sometimes that is hard because it isn't how you feel about a subject. But just because a perspective is different doesn't mean it is wrong. It also doesn't mean you have to *agree* with it. But accepting your partner's perspective helps you move forward toward making plans.

> **This is a no B.S. book.** What does that mean? It means we expect you to cut the crap. Don't blame someone else for your problems, and don't expect someone else to fix your mistakes. When you own your own stuff, you can make plans to fix it.

6. Be sensitive — We don't know too many people who truly enjoy receiving constructive criticism. Constructive or not, it is still criticism, right?!? But it is a necessary part of this process. So do your best to deliver any critiques in a loving and kind manner. If you and your partner are going to share intimate feelings, concerns, dreams, etc., you should create a caring and sensitive environment in which you both feel comfortable. Try to be as supportive and helpful as you can to each other. Be aware of your partner's feelings. We know it sounds simple, but you know where their buttons are — *DON'T PUSH THEM!*

And when you are on the receiving end, try to listen objectively to what your partner is saying. They have faults that you perceive, and you have faults that they perceive. Right now you cannot see some of these at all, so they may be pointed out to you during your retreat. Look at these as areas in which you can improve in order to make each other more comfortable in your daily lives and help you reach your goals.

7. Leave your ego in the car — There may be a lot of ego involved in many of the subjects you are going to talk about. Agreeing that someone else has a valid point might feel like you are admitting you are wrong. Try to adopt the attitude that it doesn't matter who is right if it is for the greater good of your relationship and your family. When Richard makes a good point (which is undoubtedly all too often), Amanda is known for looking at Richard, shaking her fist, and saying, "Damn it, you are right. Which is really a problem because I thought I was the only perfect person on Earth." It's her way of letting go of a little bit of her ego, but doing it with humor to lessen the sting a bit.

8. Focus on the end goal — Remember, few things in life come easy. Grammy-winning artists don't just wake up one day and decide to record a hit record — there are years of hard work and dedication that lead to success! It can be hard, painful work, but if you want to have a strong relationship, keep focusing on that end result and difficult discussions will be easier.

9. Stay committed — As we have already mentioned, this may not be easy all of the time. Some of the sections might be a cakewalk and you will revel in how well you are doing in that particular area. Other areas might be challenging. It is easy to look into the eyes of adversity but decide to stay in bed instead. We believe that these challenging areas are the reason you decided to pick up this book. Face them head on, give them the time they need, deal with the issues, and then congratulate yourself for sticking with the tough stuff.

10. Stay on task — Review your agenda before you begin a topic and set a timer if you have to. When your time is up for a topic, you are done with that topic, and done with the hard feelings that might have come up. Take a breather, and then move on.

11. Have fun — No, we are not stuttering. We have said it yet again. You are making a great commitment to be proactive by working on the very central part of yourselves and your relationship. Make this a fun process and take pride in your commitment! (Amanda really did put "having fun" into our wedding vows — she's serious about her fun!)

12. Take responsibility — When you blame someone else for something that's not going right in your own life, you throw away the key to fixing it. Once you take 100 percent responsibility, you have the means to change your life to the way you want it to be. When you don't take responsibility, you give up your power. *Responsibility* means the ability to respond. And that means you're growing in personal power and not acting like a victim, so you'll begin to see fewer instances of victimization in your life. Take responsibility and own your own power!

> **TIP:** If you're having a hard time coming to terms with something your partner is saying, write it down and think about it for a while. Sometimes just sitting with an idea makes you more comfortable and accepting. (Yes, this is what's called putting a positive spin on stewing.)

A FEW ADDITIONAL POINTS

You are participating in this retreat for yourself. There are no tests; no grades will be issued. You will know if you succeeded if you feel better at the end than you did when you started (or maybe a few weeks later). And the real excitement will be evident a few months later when you see the results of your action items moving you proactively toward your dreams and goals.

What you get out of this retreat will be in equal proportion to what you put in. If you hold back and don't do the work, you are only cheating yourselves. Actually, that's not true; you are also cheating the rest of the people who love you.

So commit to being the best people and family you can be...and while you do it all, remember to *HAVE FUN!* (Have fun, by the way, is almost a registered trademark of the Amanda Adams-Barney "corporation," if you haven't already figured that out.)

Our Story: I'm Venting Here

When we had our first fight, there was a terrible crime committed. Amanda's mom took Richard's side in the fight (and we weren't even married yet)! The subject of the fight is irrelevant, but what happened after the fight might have saved our relationship from doom.

Several days later a package arrived in the mail. The envelope contained several cards. One of them was for Amanda, and it read "I'm venting." The other cards were for Richard. There were about twenty of them, and they said things like: "That's terrible," and "They can't do that to you."

These cards were magic. They were a simple tool, but they pointed out a very big issue that was at the heart of our fight. Amanda didn't want Richard to solve her problems — she just wanted him to listen.

And while these cards are now safely tucked away in our memory box, we have never forgotten the message they conveyed. Sometimes Amanda just says "I'm venting" and Richard knows to get *out* of solution mode and *into* support mode.

Visit our website to get your very own copy of these helpful cards!

In summary, here are the twelve ground rules to retreat by:

1. Have fun

2. Everyone does all the work

3. Listen

4. Be honest

5. Be accepting

6. Be sensitive

7. Leave your ego in the car

8. Focus on the end goal

9. Stay committed

10. Stay on task

11. Have fun

12. Take responsibility

CHAPTER 6
BEING PREPARED

(What to Expect When You're
Expecting — a Retreat, That Is...)

CHAPTER 6
BEING PREPARED
(What to Expect When You're Expecting —
a Retreat, That Is…)

*"Let your boat of life be light, packed with only what you need — a homely home
and simple pleasures, one to two friends, worth the name, someone to love and
someone to love you, a cat, a dog, and a pipe or two, enough to eat and enough to
wear, and a little more than enough to drink; for thirst is a dangerous thing."*
— Jerome Klapka Jerome

OUR STORY: Ack! Is that Something New I See on the Horizon?!? (Amanda's Take)

I don't like change! Not at all, really. Not big change or little change. In fact, I think I like change as much as a lady likes an underwire bra on a 100 degree day.

But if I am going to experience something new, it always helps me to know what to expect before I go into that new situation. So this chapter is really for me and for all the people like me. Here are some of the things we have experienced over the years and what we learned to do.

Maybe if I had a list like this before our first retreat I wouldn't have been so hesitant.

If you've never done this kind of thing before, you might have a lot of different emotions. Excitement. Trepidation. Eagerness. Fear. But hopefully this information will help you feel powerful (or at least a little more comfy).

Here are some of the things you might expect during or after your retreat:

1. **You should feel reenergized** — This will come not only from the mini-vacation that you just took (who couldn't use a little time to sleep in or a nice meal out?), but also from all of the possibilities that you have identified *together*.

2. **You will have fun** — Okay, I know we are beating a dead horse here, but we really like the music on this merry-go-round (ha, ha — dead horse = merry-go-round. Get it?!?).

3. **You will have some "sexy time"** — We're not going to say any more about this except that you can just give us a high five when you meet us, for including this chapter in the book.

4. **You might have some crying, sniffling, or really strong emotions** — That's right, there might be these moments during your retreat. But if so, take it as a positive sign that you are being real with your issues and getting to the heart of the matter. And know that the subject will only last for a short period of time and then you will move on to something else.

5. **Your relationship will feel renewed and transformed** — It is easy to fall into a sense of complacency, especially when we focus on our work and kids and everyone else all day long. Taking some time to focus on your relationship allows you to remember why you loved each other in the first place.

6. **Expected times will vary wildly** — Some subjects will push well beyond the scheduled time while others will fly by. Be a bit flexible with the schedule, but getting to all of your topics is very important.

7. **You will have a long list of cool goals** — Maybe even some you never knew you wanted to achieve. Now here is the downside: You might not be able to get to all of them all at once. You *might* actually have to prioritize. But you'll have plenty of new things to try as a couple. How much fun is that?!!

8. **You might be very surprised** — Honestly inspecting your relationship and sharing with your partner leads to surprises — some of which will be significant. The *why* behind each topic is the key. And we're going to challenge you to dig deep and think hard, and then share that information with each other so you gain understanding — both through your own introspection and the feedback from your partner. This is the first step toward success.

9. **You will be exhausted at times** — Really delving into and talking about deep or difficult topics can be emotionally draining. That's why the fun times are so important — a chance to recharge your batteries.

10. **You might feel more in control of your life (rather than letting your life control you)** — We intend for you to work through this weekend and take a good stab at cutting out the crap. Eliminate the stuff that isn't working in your life to make room for the goals and dreams that you really want to accomplish together.

WHAT *NOT* TO EXPECT

Miracles — Spending one weekend working on your relationship won't all of a sudden make you "The Couple of the Year." Besides, we already think *we* own that title, so back off! (Humor.) (Sort of.) Being fabulous takes time and sustained effort. But this weekend will give you a good foundation and help isolate the areas on which you should focus your efforts.

A Walk in the Park (i.e., gain without pain) — That's right. There might be tough decisions, cross words, or even tears. (But then again, Amanda cries at commercials and YouTube videos, so perhaps she's not the best barometer.) But that's okay. Know that doing the tough work now will pay off in the end. Don't be afraid to be real and raw with your emotions. The more honest you are the more benefit you will get out of your time — and who has time to waste these days?

INTERMISSION

CHAPTER 7
CUDDLE BREAK

Chapter 7
CUDDLE BREAK

"If you're angry at a loved one, hug that person. And mean it. You may not want to hug — which is all the more reason to do so. It's hard to stay angry when someone shows they love you, and that's precisely what happens when we hug each other."

— Walter Anderson, *The Confidence Course*, 1997

That's right. Sounds corny, but we are commanding you to do it. Drop whatever you are doing right now and cuddle. Ol' fashioned snuggling. Just get right up next to each other and actually touch. Yep — whether you are reading the book for the first time or are actually on your retreat. If you are reading these words, the next thing you are doing had better be kanoodeling.

The point, you might ask? To connect. This process can be either exhilarating or challenging for people. If it is exhilarating, then this is just a chance to enjoy each other. If it is challenging, then touching each other may remind you of what is at stake and why you are doing this.

So do it! Right now.

SECTION 3
The Workbook

CHAPTER 8
USING THE WORKBOOK
(What Are We Supposed to Do with This?)

CHAPTER 8
USING THE WORKBOOK
(What Are We Supposed to Do with This?)

"When it is obvious that the goals cannot be reached, don't adjust the goals, adjust the action steps."
— Confucius

"Four steps to achievement: plan purposefully, prepare prayerfully, proceed positively, pursue persistently."
— William Arthur Ward

The rest of this book is where the rubber really meets the road. It's the heart of the matter. The real meat and potatoes of it. The core of this...okay, enough! You get the point.

In Section 1 we regaled you with the logic and stories and platitudes to convince you to buy into our retreat program. Section 2 was devoted to pre-work and what to expect before the retreat.

In Section 3 we've pulled together what we consider to be the top ten areas to cover at a retreat and provided some discussion points for working through each topic. Each of the next ten workbook chapters covers, in depth, how to approach each of the key areas of your life.

So how should you use this workbook? There really is no one right way to leverage the next several pages. It's reference, for Pete's sake — just a big ol' pile of helpful insight if you need it. But here's how you *might* want to use the workbook section:

1. Scan quickly through the chapters so you have an idea of what we've covered.

2. Review the agenda you've created (if you haven't created an agenda, now would probably be a good time, don't ya think?).

3. Decide which areas you might struggle with and dive into those parts of that particular chapter.

4. Use the advice, suggestions, and tips as needed in your prep for the retreat.

5. Refer back to the workbook *during your retreat* if you find yourselves struggling in a particular section.

6. Apply THE METHOD to each section you discuss — it will help you move from discussion to action.

7. Create your own additional topics if we didn't include them (and drop us an email so we can share them on the website).

OR, if you are a couple of Type A people:

1. Read through every single page, highlight liberally, make notes in the margins, and do absolutely *everything* we suggest.

2. Stick stringently to the brilliant agenda that you put together.

3. Address *every* single question that we have outlined in every single chapter — even if they don't apply to you.

4. Use *every bit* of the advice, suggestions, and tips we've provided.

5. Thoroughly apply *every step* of THE METHOD to each chapter you discuss.

6. Circle back to the workbook during your retreat to ensure that you have missed neither the *letter* of the law nor the *essence* of what we were trying to impart to you.

CHAPTER 9
THE METHOD FOR WORKING THROUGH EACH TOPIC

(As Tim Gunn Would Say, "Make it work!")

CHAPTER 9
THE METHOD FOR WORKING THROUGH EACH TOPIC
(As Tim Gunn Would Say, "Make it work!")

"You have to leave the city of your comfort and go into the wilderness of your intuition. What you'll discover will be wonderful. What you'll discover is yourself."
— Alan Alda

THE METHOD

One of the benefits of buying an incredibly well-written book like this by two amazingly witty and good-looking people like us is that you get the advantage of our years of experience. In writing this book we really dissected the *methods* that we have used to approach the various subjects on our agenda. (Plus we've tried some things over the years that were "el stinko" and they are, of course, not included in this book!)

What we found is that no matter the topic, we really addressed every subject in basically the same way. And at the heart of it, the objective was always the same — to find our common goals and then decide how to reach them.

The method used with each topic was to take a look inside of ourselves and determine how we felt about that subject. Then we would share that information with each other and find where the common ground was. Once the common goal was identified, we determined the proactive steps required to get to the goal. (Simple Simon, no?)

So the steps (or THE METHOD as we like to call it) for approaching each topic go something like this:

1. Do your preparation.

2. Take some individual time to do self-analysis.

3. Share with your partner (and listen).

4. Find your commonalities and differences.

5. Identify your BIG DREAMS.

6. Break your dreams down into measurable action items.

7. Rinse and repeat as needed.

In a nutshell, our super-secret method is simply about reflecting, sharing, and then putting some plans together for actually making progress toward common goals.

Simple? Maybe.

Powerful? Absolutely.

> **TIP:** Apply this method to each section of your retreat.

NOW LET'S SEE WHAT EACH OF THOSE STEPS ACTUALLY MEANS

STEP 1: Preparation — If you are Type A people like us, you will want to do some work in advance of your retreat. There is a page on our website www.48HourRetreat.com that lists all of the advance work that you can undertake if you are super ambitious. Look at these items a few weeks ahead of time so you can get together any materials that will assist you in your retreat.

If you are more relaxed (or you have decided to hold your retreat tomorrow), don't be worried. You can still have a very successful retreat. You'll just incorporate this prep work into your retreat onsite.

> **TIP:** The one item that is most important to prepare in advance is the budget work. Gather all of your current expenses, including utilities, investments, work paystubs, food, clothing, medical, gifts, travel, vacations, etc., ahead of time. See Chapter 13 for more details.

Step 2: Self-Analysis — In each workbook chapter we've provided a series of questions to guide your thinking on that subject. We put these together based on *our* needs and experiences. *You* might find that several don't apply to you or that you need to add items based on your current situation.

Before you begin each section, take a look at the questions, determine which of them you want to work through, and add any additional questions so you are both working on the same set of questions. We can't imagine why you'd *ever* want to ignore any of our brilliant questions, but we hereby release you to do just that.

Once your questions are identified, take quiet time alone to really think through the topics. Write down your responses — they don't have to be finished thoughts, but you will want notes to refer to later when you share with your partner. Challenge yourself to dig deep to determine *why* you feel a certain way about a subject, not just *what* you feel.

Step 3: Sharing and Listening — The "Active Listening" method of sharing is encouraged for your retreat. After you have done your individual work on the subject, come back together and share your thoughts and feelings with each other. One person should begin and share what their thoughts were and what changes they would like to see made. The other person should listen *quietly* and *not* give immediate feedback.

You may not agree with everything your partner is saying, and that is fine. If you think you might forget what you want to say, write it down — make notes to discuss later. But you should respectfully listen to your partner and try to take their words as an honest reflection of how they feel about the subject without adding your own interpretations. Once one person is done, the other person should take their turn. (And of course, the same rules of active listening apply.)

Step 4: Commonalities and Differences — Now is the time to give feedback and/or to ask questions. Try to *calmly* discuss what your partner has said. You are certainly NOT going to agree on everything. This is a good time to point out where you do agree and then work through the areas on which you don't agree. We recommend a *fun* tool for you to use during this time. In our house we are football fans, so we use a PENALTY FLAG. Either partner can choose to throw the penalty flag when they feel the other person isn't being truthful (don't throw it *at* your partner — we don't want anyone to lose an eye). This is a fun way for you to challenge your partner to look a little deeper and see if they have really been honest with themselves about their feelings regarding a particular subject.

Step 5: Dream Big — Write down all the BIG DREAMS you have in the particular section you are discussing — all the tough stuff you want to accomplish. This isn't the time to limit yourself because you don't think you can do it or you don't have enough money or time or whatever. *WRITE IT DOWN!* Put it on the list. Dream big. Dream perfect. You can reel it all back in the last step of the weekend.

Step 6: Action Items — Take that list of dreams and make it a reality. Break down the big items into smaller steps. Put deadlines on them (it might be days, weeks, months, or even years). Without a plan, your dreams will likely never become reality. Let us repeat: *Without a plan, your dreams will likely never become reality.* And in the end that is really what this retreat is all about — prioritizing and making your dreams reality, becoming more proactive, taking action, being the authors of your own story. So list those steps that are necessary to get you to your dreams, and then put a timeline on them.

NOTE: Not all BIG DREAMS have to be about adding something or achieving something. A BIG DREAM can be about eliminating something from your life — something like a bad habit, a toxic personality, or a draining activity. Often we achieve more by subtraction than by addition!

OUR STORY: Who Says Size Doesn't Matter? (Amanda's Take)

I really struggled when writing about using the term *Big Dreams* because some people shut down when they think something is too big to accomplish. But the word BIG is a relative term. A bee is big to an ant, but a bee is small to a person. *Your* dreams are *your* dreams. And maybe coming home to a clean kitchen every day is a really BIG dream for you (because right now your kitchen is a perpetual pig sty and you don't see how it could change). If that is your dream, then *WRITE IT DOWN* and embrace it. Figure out how to make it happen.

That is the great thing about dreams — they come in all shapes and sizes. And *you* are the ones who get to choose them! With that said, we also want you to dream BIG. Somewhere in your final list should be some things you really have to struggle to accomplish, because the bigger the dream and the harder it is to accomplish, the more you will enjoy the victory when you have it.

By now you know we are big sports fans in our house, so I will use this example: I have often been told that you excel the most when you play with/against people who are much better than you. I can tell you from personal experience that this is true. So your dreams will only grow if they are in the presence of really BIG DREAMS. Don't short yourself!

WE WANT MORE!

So what if you're working on a subject and you're doing the good work and having the good conversations, but what we've provided here just doesn't cover your issue? Or perhaps you need more information and resources about a particular subject. When we started doing our retreats we would take a huge stack of resource materials with us — relationship books, sex books, budgets, everything (we are like the Boy Scouts — we like to be prepared). But that is so seventeen years ago. Now we just have our iPads with us and we find what we need online.

But we have done you even one better. If you have a need in the middle of your retreat, go to www.48HourRetreat.com and you will find a collection of resources already vetted and compiled for you. This includes worksheets (some for free, some for a fee), websites, apps, and even printed books — yes, we believe in rockin' it old school every once in awhile.

CHAPTER 10
BEGINNING THE RETREAT
(Ladies and Gentlemen, Start Your Engines)

CHAPTER 10
BEGINNING THE RETREAT
(Ladies and Gentlemen, Start Your Engines)

"Love is not a feeling, it is a conscious decision to care for another person."
— Mark Wilkinson, Lead Pastor, Journey's Crossing

As we have already said, the goal of this whole weekend is to enhance your relationship. In order to do that you need to have a positive experience. In order to have a positive experience you need to begin in a positive way.

Voilà! We have the perfect exercise to help you set a positive tone (who would have expected that?!?). This beginning exercise will help you remember why you chose your partner in the first place, and may reveal some interesting things to your partner that they didn't know about themselves.

We realize it is often hard to transition from "real life" to "retreat life." This exercise is aimed at helping you focus on the good in your relationship and on what you are about to do to make it even better. No matter how you have constructed your retreat agenda, this should be your first exercise.

THE EULOGY

The exercise: Write a eulogy for your partner that you would deliver if they dropped dead today.

What?!

Okay, it may sound a little morbid, but trust us, it will be a good thing.

Really. You need to trust us. Okay?

Seriously; trust us and *do this!* Then send us an email at 48HourRetreat@gmail.com telling us how much you loved this exercise.

The parameters: Here are the basics of a eulogy. When someone has passed away, people who loved them get up and tell stories and make points about the person that illuminate what a great person they were. Eulogies almost always focus on the positive and gloss over the negative. And a really great eulogy makes people cry, so you might want to add tissues to your packing list.

If you are having trouble starting, write down:

- Five reasons you fell in love with your partner
- Five reasons you love your partner now
- Their five most outstanding qualities
- Your three favorite stories

From there you should be able to piece together some nice things to say that should cover three to five minutes.

Now what?

Deliver the eulogy, silly!

Have your partner stand behind you, because they wouldn't be looking at you if they were deceased, now, would they?!? Or they can lie in front of you with their arms folded and eyes closed if they want to act like a dummy — ha ha.

Now read your eulogy. Give it feeling and emotion. Allow yourself to become immersed in the feelings that you might have if your partner had just suddenly passed away. If you can't be that "real" with this exercise, at least treat the exercise with the same respect and honor you would a traditional eulogy.

This exercise should accomplish a couple of things:

1. You will look into your heart and your memory to pick out the things you really love about your partner. You will remember why you first fell in love with them and what you still love about them today. You will also recall some fond memories of times that you have shared together. It is these shared experiences that couples build on as they move forward in their lives together.

2. The demands of daily life often overtake us and we forget to appreciate our partner or tell them how much we love them. The saddest part of a eulogy is that all of these great things get said about someone after they are dead — when they can't hear them and appreciate them (all theological debates aside). This is a time for your partner to see all of the reasons you are still in love with them. Hopefully the person on the receiving end of the eulogy will gain a lasting impression of how much they are loved and acknowledge their own personal successes.

3. It will set a positive tone for the weekend. This weekend is about affirming (or reigniting) the good in your relationship, not necessarily focusing on the bad. This exercise highlights positive personal experiences that you have shared and sets a positive tone for the whole weekend.

CHAPTER 11
GOALS AND VALUES

(Are You Building on a Firm Foundation or on a Swamp?)

CHAPTER 11
GOALS AND VALUES
(Are You Building on a Firm Foundation or on a Swamp?)

"We have two kinds of morality side by side: one which we preach but do not practice and another which we practice but seldom preach."
— Bertrand Russell

OUR STORY: Identify What's Important (Richard's Take)

Examining values, setting goals, etc. are things that I initially brought to the retreat, and frankly they are things that Amanda really struggled with. Not everyone is pre-wired for examining their core beliefs or really understanding and sharing their values. However, Amanda is now a big proponent of identifying guiding principles/values/beliefs because she's seen how valuable it's become to our decision-making process as a couple.

One example is that we both agreed that developing and nurturing strong friendships was one of our top values. However, in identifying that as a value, we realized that we weren't doing everything we needed to in this category. So in retreat after retreat we've examined this value and developed goals and action plans to help support it and enhance our friendships.

Okay, here we are at the real meat of the book. This first workbook topic lays the foundation for the retreat. It is as crucial as they come. It is important because your personal values and those that you establish as a couple form the basis for making decisions for your entire family and your future. At least that is the ideal situation — you build a foundation, and then any questions that arise as time goes on can be answered by referring back to your pre-established beliefs. In case you missed it — *THIS IS VERY IMPORTANT STUFF, SO PAY ATTENTION!*

The key to this process is self-knowledge — understanding what it is that you value and believe, then taking a hard look at your goals and making sure that your goals support your beliefs and values.

For instance: If you value a strong family unit, then a personal goal of making a million-dollar salary in an extremely cutthroat industry that has you on the road all the time might be counterproductive in supporting that value. (Yikes — that is a lot of pressure. But no worries — we'll walk you through it.)

There are a host of great organizations in America that have empty mission statements meant to reflect that organization's values. A group of marketing types get together and come up with a mission statement that sounds good and will work well in marketing, promotion, PR, etc., but too often they are exercises in spin.

However, companies that spend the time and effort to really determine what they stand for and what they value can gain a huge advantage. Guiding principles from such a company help everyone in the organization know what is most important when making decisions. If really thought out and done right, knowing and living core values is crucial for organizations and individuals. The same should be true with your relationship.

Steven Covey, in his international bestseller, *The 7 Habits of Highly Effective People*, sums up this self-analysis as "beginning with the end in mind." Here's how he describes the importance:

> Each part of your life — today's behavior, tomorrow's behavior, next week's behavior, next month's behavior — can be examined in the context of the whole — of what really matters most to you. By keeping that end clearly in mind, you can make certain that whatever you do on any particular day does not violate the criteria you have defined as supremely important, and that each day of your life contributes in a meaningful way to the vision you have of your life as a whole. People often find themselves achieving victories that are empty — successes that have come at the expense of things they suddenly realize were far more valuable to them.

Most of us are just trying to get through the day or week. Let's face it — coming up with a list of values and a mission statement is a daunting task for a lot of us. However, to really make this retreat, your marriage, and your life as successful and fulfilling as you want it to be, the first step is to take the time to examine what's most important to you — both individually and as a couple. This means some quiet time in introspection, thinking about what is most important to you. It involves hard work and muscles we don't use often. Initially this should be done individually and then merged into values and goals for your family.

We're serious about your getting serious here, so follow these steps and DO IT!

TIME TO START DOING THE WORK — APPLY "THE METHOD"

Since this is the first working topic on your retreat agenda, we are going to walk you through how to apply THE METHOD to this section. We won't do this for every section — we know you are smart and can figure it out on your own. But we thought we would give you an example so you can see how we suggest using THE METHOD.

In each workbook chapter we present questions and issues that are beginnings for your consideration as you work through the self-analysis step of THE METHOD.

STEP 1 — SELF-ANALYSIS

Identify your values — Values are the core *teachings* and *beliefs* that make you who you are. Most of us were taught values by our family and/or our religion. What are the basic principles of your life that shape who you are? What principles do you hold most dear? Develop your own list of values and share it with your partner. You should feel free to ask your partner to explain a value and how it applies. Do this in a loving and non-threatening way, in the vein of learning more about your partner and what makes them tick. If you need help finding words that fit the values you have, you can visit our website at www.48HourRetreat.com and there you will find some ideas to help you come up with your own list.

Write your personal mission statement — If you talk with people who have become successful, there is often one common thread: They knew what they wanted to do. Companies develop mission statements so they know where they are going, and so should you. Take some time to really think about who you are, what you want to accomplish in your life, and what will make you happy. Now write your own mission statement. It does not need to be long or elaborate, but it should support your values. Each person should develop their own statement and then share the statement with their partner. This mission statement is best written in the affirmative "I am…" format.

> ## An example of Richard's mission statement from several years ago was:
>
> I am a happy person who tries to live my life by God's principles and with his guidance. I am an active parent, a person who nurtures his friendships, and a spouse who continually works to improve his marriage. I am always seeking self-improvement and I give back my time and talents to my community.

Create a "bucket list" for yourself — This is a list of items you really want to do before you "kick the bucket." Think about how you apply your values to your everyday life and how you are going to fulfill your mission statement. Create a bucket list for yourself. There may be things on your list you do just for yourself, and there may be things you do with your partner and/or family. Think BIG lifelong dreams. The following are some areas you might want to consider for defining items for your bucket list:

— Career

— Community Service

— Faith/Spirituality

— Family

— Physical Well-Being

— Travel

WHAT TO DO NEXT?
STEP 2 — SHARE AND LISTEN

The next step in THE METHOD is to **share (and listen)** with your partner. Typically this step is implicit in the self-analysis. Once you think about the subject at hand individually, then you share what you have learned with each other.

In this case it means sharing with each other your list of values, your personal mission statements, and your bucket lists. One person goes first and shares, then the other person reads what they have come up with.

STEP 3 — COMMONALITIES AND DIFFERENCES

Now identify your **commonalities** and **differences**. In the example of goals and values, you might discuss where there is overlap and where your lists diverge. Are there things that you want to add to your list based on your partner's reactions? Are there areas about which you need to agree to disagree (but still respect and support each other's perspectives)?

STEP 4 — LET YOUR IMAGINATION RUN WILD

The next step is usually the fun, juicy one — it is to identify your BIG DREAMS. For this example, you have done that individually when you prepared your bucket lists. But now you should form a couple and/or family bucket list. What do you want to do together? Do you have goals and dreams for your family that are greater than what you can accomplish alone? Write it all down. Don't limit yourself. Enjoy the possibilities. Deal with the reality later in the retreat.

STEP 5 — MAKE IT HAPPEN!

Now that you know *where* you want to go, break it down into the *how* you're going to get there part. Create a set of *action items* for yourselves — a road map, if you will, of how you will get to your BIG DREAMS. Take your bucket list and put some dates on it. When will you do things? Do you have to do other things (like make money or get more education) in order to accomplish anything on your list? Identify what you need and when you need it in order to make your BIG DREAMS reality.

And that is it! Applying THE METHOD to any particular section is as easy as that.

OUR STORY: I Don't Care if You're a Tough Mudder ...Or Do I?!? (Amanda's Take)

Often what people think is, "I have one goal, my partner has a different goal, and now it becomes about whose goal is more important." Instead, there could be something that is important to Richard that might not be as important to me, but we both commit to it.

For instance, Richard signed up for this stupid race. The Tough Mudder — twelve miles going through mud and over walls. It's completely testosterone-laden. In some respects I was totally thrilled that he was doing it because it was helping his fitness level, which is one of the big things on his list of goals, and supported his core value of focusing on good health.

I wasn't running the race; it wasn't my goal; I didn't care. But I knew that it was his goal and I should support it, and therefore, on the weekends, when we might otherwise be doing something else, he said, "No, I've got to make time to train for the race." I thought, "Okay, the choice for this amount of time is either we do something together or he's training, but he has this goal and it's important so he's training. We'll do something together later, and when we do he will be happier because he is moving toward his goal."

And if Richard is happy, then everyone in the household is happier.

THE SHORT AND SNAPPY SUMMARY OF OUR BRILLIANT DISCUSSION POINTS:

- Identify your values.

- Write your personal mission statement.

- Create a bucket list for yourself.

- Apply THE METHOD.

- Identify your BIG DREAMS.

- Create your action plans to get you where you want to go.

CHAPTER 12
RELATIONSHIP
(Just You and Me)

CHAPTER 12
RELATIONSHIP
(Just You and Me)

"It's a helluva start, being able to recognize what makes you happy."
— Lucille Ball

Your relationship is what the whole weekend is about, right? So why a *separate* chapter titled "Relationship"?

The whole weekend is about the various components of you, your relationship, and your life together. But there needs to be some time devoted directly to how the two of you relate to each other and work together. Included here are some discussion points that will help set the stage for much of the work that you're going to be doing for the rest of the weekend. This subject can be a bit tender sometimes, but trust us, it is better to get things out there than to just let them fester.

We have also gathered a collection of our solutions to relationship issues over the years and we just couldn't resist sprinkling them into this chapter. They are included right among the self-analysis activities. You're welcome!

SELF-ANALYSIS

State of the union — What do you feel is the current state of your relationship? Much like the President, spend some time giving a speech. (Yes, we are fond of giving speeches — just ask our kids, they will tell you.) Tell your partner what you feel are the good points about your *relationship* (this is different from the eulogy you did of your partner because this exercise focuses on your union). Really try to think about what you enjoy. Each person should give their own speech. In this part of the exercise you focus *only on the areas that are working* — there will be time for improvement suggestions later.

Why are you here? (At this retreat, not here on Earth — hopefully you did that in the values discussion.) Consider these questions:

- What do you want to accomplish?

- What do you think is realistic?

- What are the barriers to achieving these goals?

- How can you help your partner achieve their goals?

- How can they help you achieve your goals?

Try to be as concrete as possible when answering these questions so you have a good idea about what each of you hopes to get out of your retreat.

> **TIP:** Arguably at the root of most relationship problems is the ability (or lack of it) to communicate with each other. If you struggle with this area, we recommend *The Seven Principles for Making Marriage Work* by John Gottman and Nan Silver. Communication skills are like muscles, if you don't use them, you will lose them. So start some exercises today, but then make a commitment to keep doing refresher courses on a regular basis.

Expectations — Expectations are sometimes our worst enemy. Unmet expectations mean disappointment, sadness, and sometimes even resentment. The problem with expectations is that they often go unvoiced. We create expectations for other people, don't express them, and are then let down when those people don't meet our silent expectations. Have you ever really expressed your expectations to your partner? Do you assume they know what you want and need from them? Is this all too touchy-feely already? Suck it up — this is a *relationship* retreat!

Write a list of ten expectations you have of your partner (*realistic* expectations, people). Now share the list with your partner. Have an open discussion about the lists. Are there things on your partner's list that you didn't know they were expecting of you? Are there things you don't feel you can deliver? This list should help you identify the issues that are important for your partner and help you better provide for your partner.

Your own time versus together time (demands versus desires) — Did you ever have a houseguest who overstayed their welcome? (Richard's mom strictly adheres to the "fish and houseguests stink after three days" rule.) Well, sometimes living with a partner can feel the same way. It is very normal for people to desire differing levels of time with each other. This is another area in which communication is the key to success. And the key here is not to talk the time issue to death, but rather to discuss the emotions that are related to the time issue.

SOLUTION CENTER: We hope that you can work toward a compromise solution that meets both of your needs. Often, where time is concerned, we know that a "you scratch my back, I'll scratch yours" approach works. For instance, if I happily and willingly "let" my husband go play golf on Saturday morning, then he is much happier to spend the afternoon doing something with me that I want to do. In this case, we both get something we want, and it is even better because everyone was happy about it.

WARNING: Don't fall into a chit hole (get it? ha, ha). It will not do you any good to keep a chart (literal or mental) of "points" each of you is "spending." We can tell you from experience that rarely do two people assign the same point value to different activities.

Attitude adjustment — One of the things that affects Richard the most is Amanda's attitude. (Amanda wishes it weren't true, but the old saying "If Momma ain't happy, ain't nobody happy" definitely holds up in our house.) And the reverse also applies (though to a lesser degree). If Richard comes through the door at the end of a workday in a foul mood, that can ruin Amanda's entire evening. It is time to do a little work and see what is really going on with your mood each day. You can find a Mood Journal Exercise on our website that will help you identify your mood triggers, so you can begin to manage your triggers and therefore improve your mood.

SOLUTION CENTER: People choose different ways to deal with stress. If one partner had a stressful day or got stuck in traffic, they might not want to be peppered with questions or asked to do chores as soon as they step through the doorway. They might need some "me" time. This could be accomplished in as little as ten or fifteen minutes. Ask your partner if this would be beneficial. Often when we have even just a bit of time to ourselves we feel complete and ready for social interaction instead of feeling robbed of time or put-upon or "slammed." Taking time for a run or to get changed into comfortable clothes and decompress in a lounge chair can do wonders. If you are the one getting the down time, just remember to stick to your established time limits and re-engage with your family when you promised.

Come on, we're all friends here — A good foundation for a marriage is a strong friendship (and an endless supply of alcohol, but we'll focus on the friendship for now). We can sometimes get so caught up in the day-to-day stuff of life that we forget to do the fun things that we used to do with our partner that first brought us together. And if you didn't have fun together to begin with, then now is the time to start! Do our Interest Inventory Exercise (on our website) to help identify where your interests overlap.

SOLUTION CENTER: "Ugh!" you say. "There is nothing on my list that is on my partner's list." This is where compromise comes in. Amanda's mom and dad are very different people and they have very different hobbies. Amanda's mom likes the theatre. Amanda's dad likes to ride dirt bikes. There isn't much commonality there. But they love each other and truly care about what the other person is interested in. So Amanda's mom cooks meals for the guys when they come back from a ride and listens to all of their war stories. And Amanda's dad has actually gone to a Broadway show or two. Of course her mom picked her battles. She didn't ask her husband to sit through an opera; she knows he likes rock music, so she took him to a production of The Who's *Tommy*.

In the end it isn't about *loving* everything you're doing with your partner. It is about having shared experiences together that you can refer back to later. If you can love it, that is a bonus!

Fight club — Do an analysis of how you fight. That's right. Talk about it. And now, not when you're doing it. Presumably right now you aren't fighting, and that is the best time to talk about how and why you fight. When you're in the middle of a conflict you are too heated up to stop and think about strategies that would be more helpful.

SOLUTION CENTER: One of the keys to changing behavior is to recognize the behavior. Sounds simple, but sometimes it is hard to do. If you can identify the bad habits you have when you fight, then you can start to change them. This is a *process*, and it can be frustrating. The next fight you have, you might fall back into the same traps and not realize it until *after* the fact. But slowly, over time, you will begin to see the traps you're headed for in advance, and then you can ward them off and replace them with better behaviors. Here are some keys to *good* fights:

- Diffuse situations with humor.

- Believe your partner when they say "sorry."

- Be kind to each other.

- Not everything has to be said.

- Never involve your mother-in-law (long story).

REMEMBER: After you do the self-analysis, don't forget to employ the other steps in THE METHOD (see Chapter 9 for the steps in THE METHOD).

> ## OUR STORY: It's Not How Much, It's When
>
> Richard is famous for his thoughtfulness in the way he uses his time. He loves his job, and it often requires more than a forty-hour work week. What is unique is when he chooses to do his overtime. He gets up early or stays late on nights when he was already scheduled to work late. The point is that he chooses times that have the least impact on our family. The return for him is that when he does have to work a weekend or go out of town, Amanda is much more supportive because she knows Richard is very conscious of the family's time and feelings. This is a real win-win in our household!

THE SHORT AND SNAPPY SUMMARY OF OUR BRILLIANT DISCUSSION POINTS:

- What is your current state of the union?

- Why are you here (at this retreat)?

- What are your expectations of each other?

- What are your views about how much time you spend on your own versus time you spend together (demands versus desires)?

- Does anyone need an attitude adjustment?

- Do you have shared interests or activities?

- How can you fight better?

- Apply THE METHOD to ensure that you have action items to reinforce your good work.

CHAPTER 13
FINANCES
(Money Makes the World Go Round)

CHAPTER 13
FINANCES
(Money Makes the World Go Round)

"My problem lies in reconciling my gross habits with my net income."
— Errol Flynn

During our early retreats, there were always tears when it came to one subject, and that was money. That was a subject that Amanda never felt comfortable talking about. But the retreat was the best place to talk about it. We talked about saving and life insurance and goal-setting and budgeting. Richard would whip out a budget and Amanda would cry before the discussion had even begun. But then we'd talk through it and it would end up being okay.

OUR STORY: The Car Incident

AMANDA: In the beginning Richard and I had different perspectives about money, and I was fearful that since we came from such different backgrounds we were going to have big arguments about it.

RICHARD: What illuminated our different outlooks was "the car incident" that happened before we were married. Amanda's car needed repairs, so while she was away I took her car to the shop. I spent more money on it than Amanda would have spent. There were a few things that had to be done right then, and there were other things that I decided would be prudent to do sooner rather than later.

continued

AMANDA: When I got back and found out that he had done this "nice" but expensive gesture, I was steaming mad. Why would I be mad about his doing something nice? When I had a chance to think about it I realized that I was really petrified that he was going to find out that I was not fiscally responsible and couldn't afford the repairs on my car. In my mind he was so fiscally prudent that if he found out I wasn't, he wasn't going to like me anymore.

RICHARD: The funniest part—as has always been the case with pretty much everything — was that once we talked about it, I said, "What are you talking about? Number one, I have not always been that fiscally prudent, and number two, I still like you. We're good… it's okay. Nobody's perfect…everything's fine."

AMANDA: This is one of the reasons a retreat works for us. We fear the things that we don't know about. I had all these presumptions about how Richard was going to react about finances — and in reality once we talked about it, it wasn't nearly like my fears made it out to be.

At one time this chapter was entitled "Budgeting." But then we realized that even the mere mention of this word would make some of you skip right over the chapter and move on to something more appealing (say sex, perhaps). For most couples (except those who are independently wealthy — and rumor has it that even they might struggle with this issue), this is often the area of greatest conflict in their relationship.

Usually the way it goes is that you have limited funds and have to work to keep your spending in line with those funds — at least that is the goal. And generally one person spends more and the other person nags about the spending. This sets up a point of conflict.

Sometimes a couple's ideas about money are diametrically opposed. And money, let's face it, is something we encounter pretty much every day of our lives, from buying a cup of coffee to paying the mortgage.

So depending on your perspectives in your relationship, here are some scenarios:

— Both partners spend freely.

— Both partners are careful with their money.

— One partner spends, the other is careful.

— One partner spends on certain things, the other is careful with money on specific items and this flip-flops all the time.

You can see how in every case it would be beneficial to have discussions and planning to help both partners feel good about their money and financial future. (Unless, of course, you're ridiculously wealthy!)

Therefore no retreat can happen without a discussion about money, as much as Amanda may wish it was not so. We have actually included two discussions about money. (We know that this may seem daunting, but really there is a method to the madness.) We feel that it is necessary to begin the weekend by talking about money. This accomplishes two things: 1) it gets the big hairy monster out of the way, and 2) it gives you some guidelines for the rest of the weekend. When you are done with this chapter you should have a better feeling for where your current state of affairs lies (you won't be *guessing*...if you do the work you will *know*).

While you go through the rest of the agenda, do not eliminate anything because of your current monetary situation, merely write down the issue or goal and put it in the budget file. At the end of the weekend you are going to come back to the budget. Once you have a better understanding of yourselves, your individual goals, and your goals as a couple, it will be time to take another look at your budget. Maybe things have changed — things that were important at the beginning of the weekend are no longer as important, or *maybe* you want to work a little harder to make room in the budget for your new joint priorities.

This second look at your finances (at the end of the retreat) is a time to incorporate your new dreams and plans for the future into the budget. These might not be goals you reach in the next six months, but you can start planning now for the long haul. And even Amanda, who used to be a "deal with things as they come" type of person, can see the benefit of budgeting now. Richard is so proud!

> **TIP:** This is the prep work we most strongly suggest you do in advance. Gather all of your current expenses, including utilities, investments, work paystubs, food, clothing, medical, gifts, travel, vacations, etc. Try to get an accurate handle on your income and expenses before you leave on your retreat so you can have a productive financial discussion.

SELF-ANALYSIS

Money and emotion — Before you do any planning, it's a good idea to get the emotional aspect of money out in the open (obviously budgeting has scarred Amanda for life). Here are some questions to work on individually and then discuss with your partner:

1. What does money represent to you? For example, it could mean freedom or it could mean self-esteem in that you can take care of yourself and your family very well.

2. What does lack of money represent to you?

3. What kinds of emotions does lack of money bring up? Write them down — even if they don't seem logical or rational.

4. In your family, what kinds of gifts were given for birthdays, holidays, graduations, and anniversaries?

5. How do you feel when you get a gift or celebrate an anniversary with your partner? Shortchanged? Slighted? Or do you feel loved and cared for?

6. What would you most like to do with money in general? For example, spending on the house versus travel, children's education, your own continuing education or new business, helping out your parents, starting a non-profit, retirement, savings, etc.

7. Where in your yard do you plan on planting that money tree? (humor, ha ha)

Financial background — If you have never discussed your financial background with your partner, now is the time. Actually the time was probably years ago, so you might want to dive in now. Understand where each of you is coming from. Did your parents "rob Peter to pay Paul," or were they completely conservative with their financial matters? Have you had credit problems in the past, or is your record squeaky clean? All of these issues have created your current attitudes toward money, and you each should understand this background.

You Just Won the Publisher's Clearing House Sweepstakes! Perhaps you have dreamed and schemed about what you would do with ten million dollars if you won the lottery. Or maybe you aren't the type to spend your money that way, so the thought has never occurred to you. Your propensity to play the lottery or not is not actually important to this exercise. Just pretend that you *have* hit the lottery and you get a take-home payout of ten million dollars (after taxes are paid, etc.). What would you do with it? Would you save it or spend it? Would you share it with family and friends? If so, how would you spend and share it; and if you're going to save it, what are you saving for? Each of you should make up your own list of ways in which you would allocate the money (yes, account for every last dollar), and then share your accounting with each other. This exercise can help illuminate some similarities and differences in your financial approaches.

Current financial status — Crunch those numbers (if you have done this in advance, good for you)! Organize all of your information into a spreadsheet and get a feel for where your money goes. Do you agree on how your money is currently being spent? Are there changes that need to be made? What are those adjustments?

Spending guidelines — Once you have determined what changes need to be made, try to agree on exactly how the money is going to be spent. What are your priorities, and how much will you give to them?

What's that?!? You think this sounds like a budget? Well, perhaps you are right. But the idea of *spending guidelines* feels much more comfortable to Amanda (a self-confessed budget hater). With spending guidelines, she feels like she is in charge. She knows about where she wants to be each month, and she knows that she has options. If our son wants the latest (expensive) basketball shoes, and she wants to be the cool mom and buy them for him, she can do that and forgo the new top for herself she was going to buy. It is all a matter of perspective, and somehow when she is making her own decisions and owning our financial future, she is much more okay with it. Try it — spending guidelines, not a budget — you might like it!

> **TIP:** Set up your bills to be paid automatically or online. This avoids late fees and saves you time and money.

Investments/savings plan — More and more these days we are being informed that we need to save for our own future and retirement. Assess what you need for your retirement, what you are currently saving, and what your goals are. It is never too soon to talk to a financial planner. Find a planner who will work with you in the early phases of your saving to put together a plan. Even if you don't have any money to invest, a good planner will start working with you now and tell you what you should have prior to investing. A good planner can also analyze your current insurance situation and let you know what types of insurance you require. Be sure that you work with a certified financial planner — they are more than just brokers and can take a look at your entire financial picture.

You probably didn't bring a financial planner with you on your retreat, but you *can* add "find a financial planner" to your goals!

Wills and organ donation — Boy, this is really turning out to be the fun chapter, huh? If budgets aren't exciting enough, now we're going to talk about dying!

If you already have a will and have all your financial papers organized, you can to go the head of the class. But if your will is more than five years old, you will want to get it out and review it. Make sure that you both agree about all of the decisions you made and make any changes that might need to be made. (For instance, you no longer talk to your "best friends" whom you asked to be guardians of your children.) If minor changes are needed, a quick call to an attorney should take care of them. For more extensive changes, a sit-down might be necessary.

Unfortunately, you are probably one of the couples who don't have a will. How do we know this? The reality is that up to seven out of ten people have not drawn up a will.

Thousands of (likely boring) books have been written on the topic, and this is clearly not something you are going to get done during the weekend (that is, unless you had the forethought to bring an attorney with you). What you can do, however, is discuss the issues that need to be addressed in your will so you are prepared when you meet with someone to draw up the papers. We have a worksheet on our website that covers questions that are commonly asked when preparing a will.

Insurance — Whether renting or owning a home, you need insurance for your "stuff," and likely life insurance. The amounts and types of insurance you need vary depending on your ages, your assets, and the ability of your partner to work should you die or become disabled. This is another item that you are not going to complete while you are on your retreat (unless, of course, that attorney you brought along also sells insurance), but you can put it on the to-do list for when you return home.

ALTERNATIVE: If all this sounds difficult, you could always just put your fingers in your ears and run around yelling "La, la, la, I can't hear you! I want candy now!"

TIP: Make sure to put something fun or light on the agenda after budget discussions. Or maybe a champagne toast if that works for you! This section can be tough, but you should feel a sense of accomplishment when it is done!

OUR STORY: Tighten that Belt (Richard's Take)

One of the best things to come out of one of our early retreats was our commitment to buy our first house. Coming up with a down payment was going to be a challenge for us, especially at our current rate of saving. So we agreed, as a couple, that this was our number one goal and that we were both totally committed to it. Together we put together a plan for getting there that involved some very tough choices — what we took to calling our "severe austerity plan." We won't get into all the details, but together we identified dozens of very specific things we could do, from curtailing eating out to postponing most spending, foregoing any vacations, etc.

Because we had come up with plan *together* and it was at the top of our priority list, we were able to save up the money we needed in about fourteen months. We scrimped and saved everywhere, but it didn't seem so bad because we were both in it together. Working together toward an agreed-upon common goal made the sacrifices much less daunting. We saved up the money we needed, got our first home, and ended the austerity program feeling very proud of our efforts.

THE SHORT AND SNAPPY SUMMARY OF OUR BRILLIANT DISCUSSION POINTS:

- What is your emotional involvement with money?

- What is your financial background from childhood?

- What would you do if you just won the Publisher's Clearing House Sweepstakes?

- What is your current financial status?

- Do you have a household budget?

- What is your plan for investing and saving?

- Do you need to write your will?

- Do you have enough and the right types of insurance?

- Did you apply THE METHOD?

CHAPTER 14
CAREERS
(It's All in a Day's Work)

CHAPTER 14
CAREERS
(It's All in a Day's Work)

"Opportunity is missed by most people because it is dressed in overalls and looks like work."

— Thomas A. Edison

OUR STORY: Here I Go Again on My Own (Richard's Take)

The events management business that Amanda owns and has been running now for about fourteen years came out of a very proactive planning choice dealing with BIG family goals. One of our biggest goals we agreed on early in our relationship was that when we had kids, one of us could be able to stay home with them. And then we looked at who had a career that was more likely to lend itself to that in terms of income and flexibility.

Amanda was employed as a meeting planner at the time in a regular nine-to-five office job, and we decided that if she went out on her own, she could work from home and be home with the kids. But she needed to be established *before* we had kids. She couldn't have kids and then hang out her shingle the next week. About three years before we had our first child, Amanda went into business for herself and our plan has pretty much worked out perfectly — not always the way we thought it would, but usually the way it needed to.

According to the Organization for Economic Cooperation and Development, the average American spends 1,787 hours a year working — that is a lot! (At least that is how much time we're on the job. Actually working? Well….) And that is why the subject of your careers is included in the suggested agenda for your retreat. If you are going to spend that much of your life doing something, it would be great if you could enjoy it or at least get something out of it!

This is another area in which we often fall into a rut of complacency. We get in a job and get comfortable. And then we are completely surprised (and unprepared) when our company has layoffs and we are out the door. A yearly monitoring of your career path can help you proactively stay on top of your game, identify areas of career growth, and put you on a path to professional happiness.

SELF-ANALYSIS

Your current career — Take a look at your CROI (Career Return on Investment — we just made that up!). Are you getting a return from your job that is in proportion to what you are putting in? Talk about what is going on at your job right now. Are you happy? Are you unhappy? What are the good things about your job? What gives you satisfaction? What makes you happy and what do you like? Conversely, what is frustrating you? How is your job affecting you in your home life?

Career forecast — Okay, what to do now? Do you stay the course? Do you need or want to shake things up? If you want a change, how are you going to make that happen? What will a change mean for your relationship? Will you work more or less, will you make more money or less, will you need more training? How does your commute figure in? Look into your future and see what would make you happy.

Maybe there is a change coming that isn't of your choosing (layoff, business closing, etc.). How can you start preparing for that now? Maybe you are finally ready to take that great step after completing your education. What does the future look like?

Continuing education — Do either of you need or desire more education? If so, how will it affect your relationship and your schedule? When is the correct time for you to begin schooling or working with a mentor?

Keeping up with your network — The time to make and cultivate contacts is *not* when you need a job. Part of your ongoing professional development should be to continue to foster your connections. Put together a plan for how you might strengthen the professional relationships you already have and develop new ones.

Do you feel your partner is supportive of your career? What things could they do differently that would make a positive impact on your work situation?

If you were to make changes in your career, what effects can you anticipate they would have on your life and your family? Answering this question can point out the long-term positive effects that might make some short-term discomfort more palatable.

OUR STORY: You've Got It in the Palm of Your Hand

There is no greater example of our retreat at work in our lives than the very book you have in your hand. And not for the obvious reason that we started doing retreats and are now telling you how to do them, but rather the idea of turning our retreat into a book that would then become an opportunity to reach out to other couples and help them transform their relationships. That idea started at one of our retreats *many* years ago. In fact, we found a book-writing calendar from 2003!

continued

In the many years it took to bring this book to publication, it has been watched over and nurtured and grown and supported in our retreats. It has been talked about and written and lived.

What started as Amanda's goal has grown to become *our* goal. And now this is more than just a dream of writing a book. It is a BIG DREAM of creating a whole community around the book as well as opportunities for us to travel *together* and speak to other couples and share a passion that might be the next career for at least one of us.

In many more ways than one, this book wouldn't be possible if it weren't for our retreats.

THE SHORT AND SNAPPY SUMMARY OF OUR BRILLIANT DISCUSSION POINTS:

- What is your analysis of your current career situation?
- What does the forecast look like for you in your work?
- Do you need additional continuing education?
- Do you have a professional networking plan?
- How can your partner support you in your career?
- What would happen if you made a change in your career?
- What are the outcomes and plans from applying THE METHOD?

CHAPTER 15
SPIRITUALITY
(You Gotta Have Faith)

CHAPTER 15
SPIRITUALITY
(You Gotta Have Faith)

"And now these three remain: faith, hope and love. But the greatest of these is love."
— The Bible, 1 Corinthians 13:13

OUR STORY: Am I Even Qualified to Write This? (Amanda's Take)

I feel funny writing this chapter because when Richard and I first met I hadn't been to church in many years (with the exception of the occasional Christmas Eve service). While my grandmother was a very Christian woman, I was raised in a household where going to church wasn't as important as leading a good life. Meanwhile, Richard was very much raised in the church — he was an active member of the youth group, went on church mission trips, and was even a deacon while in high school.

When we got together we were in very different places in our faith journeys. But I will give all credit to my husband for being a very open and patient man. He didn't force me to go to church; he merely presented me with the opportunities and told me that he would love to have me go with him if I wanted to.

continued

And when I finally did show interest, he remained flexible about finding a church and type of service that would interest both of us. We kissed a lot of Biblical frogs, but we finally found our Prince. And through that process I found a patient and loving God who met me where I was; one who didn't need me to come from the perfect background or be a Biblical scholar.

The lesson we learned is that we needed to "find our fit"! And it wasn't just what fit for one of us. We found a place where we are all comfortable. (As our children got older and could actually participate in worship it was important that they enjoyed the experience as well.)

We all question! Sometimes you think you are the only one, but you are not. We have never met a pastor or a rabbi (or probably an imam, but we've never personally spoken to one) who said they knew their path, mission, or faith felt right *every* moment of *every* day of their lives. And we have never had a faithful friend who hasn't had a moment of doubt. That makes you wonder, "How am I supposed to know? How am I supposed to believe? If the people who are IN THE KNOW aren't sure, how can I be sure?"

Well, that is where faith comes in. And that is where a community comes in. And that is why we go to church — to find a community of other people who are learning together and investigating and figuring it out.

But we believe that the key is to find what works for you. When we were contemplating this chapter, Amanda was talking with a trusted advisor*, and through the course of our conversation he said that you need to "find your fit," and that rang so true for her.

*In full disclosure the "trusted advisor" was Amanda's cousin Jeffrey. He is no man of the cloth, but he is very smart, and certainly spoke the truth that evening.

Many of us were raised in a certain belief system. Perhaps it was the Catholic Church with confession and kneeling and the rosary, but that doesn't resonate for you now. Or perhaps you were raised Jewish, but now that you are a grown adult the religious teachings don't work for you even though you would like to retain your historical heritage.

It seems the subject of faith was much more easily approached many years ago. When we were growing up, you either were a believer or you weren't, and the number of couples who had different faiths within their relationship was much smaller than it is today.

Today our society is more open and accepting, and therefore we have more mixed-faith relationships. The General Social Survey reported that 15 percent of U.S. households were mixed faith in 1988, which grew to 25 percent in 2006 and is still increasing in number today. Obviously this requires a certain amount of understanding and compromise in order to make sure everyone's spiritual desires are met.

In the Bible's New Testament, Paul links faith, hope, and love together, and that is not a mistake. These three tenets are central to a successful relationship. Where we are strong in our faith, it feeds our love; and where our faith and our love intersect, we can find great hope (and in fact inspiration that we can accomplish more things together than we can apart).

> **NOTE:** We *fully* admit that we come to this chapter from a Judeo-Christian perspective. That is because that is how we were raised. But that doesn't mean this chapter doesn't apply to people of all faiths. Take these questions and adapt and expand them to apply to your faith journey. This is probably one of the most personal chapters in the book, so you need to *MAKE IT YOUR OWN.*

SELF-ANALYSIS

Where are you in your faith journey? Spirituality often coincides with values and goals. If you haven't discussed your personal beliefs about religion, spiritual beliefs, or church attendance, do so now. Sit down and have an honest discussion — if you don't know exactly how you feel, that is okay; just say so.

Faith in action — In keeping with the entire theme of *The 48 Hour Relationship Retreat*, you should first determine what's most important to you as an individual/couple/family when it comes to faith, then decide what you plan to do about making those important items a reality.

SOLUTION CENTER:
Some suggestions for action plans:

- Finding a place of worship
- Getting more involved with your current faith community
- Reading more about your faith, meditating, or studying your Bible, Koran, etc.
- Joining a study group to help deepen your faith
- Providing more support (financial, time, etc.) to your faith
- Finding a way to reflect on your faith more during everyday life
- Creating your own religion that revolves around sleeping in late and lots of fried foods

Children — If you have children, have you discussed how you're going to raise them in the faith community? Do you both have the same opinion? Are you sure? What are you doing to provide for their spiritual education? Do your children see you "walking the walk?"

What does *success* look like as it pertains to your faith? Is it a feeling of peace? Is it knowing the Bible well? Is it finding a faith community? Perhaps it seems a weird concept to identify goals and action plans for your faith, but there is nothing wrong with wanting to improve your spirituality. Once you know what kind of spiritual person you want to be, it is much easier to make a plan to become that person. Consider what your BIG DREAMS might be as they relate to your faith. And what it means for you in your relationship if you and your partner do not share the same goals.

OUR STORY: Men's Group (Richard's Take)

Coming out of one of our retreats I identified the need to find some type of fellowship group to help me grow in my faith. The church that we were attending at the time just happened to have a men's Bible study group on Friday mornings that perfectly fit into my schedule. This filled a real need in my life and was a fabulous part of each week for me.

Amanda thinks that this story, while appropriate, doesn't really "zing" (whatever that means). I think she just likes to tell very long stories and I like to get to the point. I think the story makes the point and doesn't need embellishment. So I'm not changing it!

TIP: Maybe when you started to apply THE METHOD to your faith discussion you didn't think there would be any action items or BIG DREAMS here, but we hope that you found areas where you can make some changes and see a difference in your life.

THE SHORT AND SNAPPY SUMMARY OF OUR BRILLIANT DISCUSSION POINTS:

- Where are you in your faith journey?
- How can you put your faith into action?
- How can you support your children in their faith journeys?
- How do you define *success* within your spiritual pursuits?
- Record your BIG DREAMS and action steps.

CHAPTER 16
HEALTH AND WELLNESS
(I Feel Good!)

CHAPTER 16
HEALTH AND WELLNESS
(I Feel Good!)

"Health is a state of complete physical, mental and social well-being, and not merely the absence of disease or infirmity."
— World Health Organization, 1948

Not Really Our Story, But a Cute Anecdote (Amanda's Take)

When I was little and I would leave my grandmother's house, I would always say, "See you soon, Grandma," and she would always answer, "Good Lord willin' and the crick don't rise." My grandma didn't live near a riverbed, so I don't think she was worried about a flood. What I do think she meant was that if the Lord granted her another day on the Earth, then she would be pleased. All the money in the world is no good if you're not around to enjoy it.

As a country we are very unhealthy. Don't believe it? Here are some stats to back us up:

According to the website NationMaster.com, the United States is first in obesity rates out of twenty-eight industrialized nations at 30.6 percent. Second was Mexico at 24.2 percent, followed by the U.K. at 23 percent. Japan was the healthiest at 3.2 percent. According to the 2011 Center for Disease Control's annual report on health statistics, "Fewer than two in 10 Americans get the recommended levels of exercise, and more than ¼ of U.S. adults do not devote any time to physical activity."

Even if your weight falls in the healthy range, are you doing all that you should to maintain your best level of fitness (so you can do everything you want to do)?

HEY! Put down those Oreos and pay attention, buster! This health thing is important.

Just because you are not sick today doesn't mean you are healthy, and even though you might be fit, you might be lacking nutrients or essentials in your diet. It's time to dig deep and do an honest assessment of your health. It's either that or you can plan on complaining endlessly to all who will listen about your myriad of ailments as you get older!

SELF-ANALYSIS

As the quote that opened the chapter reminds us, health isn't just one thing; it is a multi-faceted area that combines many elements of our lives. Use these questions to think about your overall health and well-being. You can choose to answer each question individually, or choose instead to use these as a guide and write your own summary of your current health status. Either way it is time to take yourself in for an overall physical (even if only in the metaphorical sense).

How do you feel about your current health status? What were the messages you were given about being healthy when you were growing up? Was health (both physical and mental) important to your parents? If you are in good health, what motivates you to stay that way; if you are not, what keeps you from making positive changes? Do you feel you are as healthy as you could be? Is your bathroom scale mocking you?

How does your current health condition affect your everyday life? Is your current health status a supporting factor in your overall happiness, or a deterrent to your success?

Are there specific areas in your life that would be better if your overall health were to improve? When we are overweight we generally don't feel sexy at all (we don't want anyone to see our rolls of fat — even our partner), and our sex lives suffer. And it is sure easier to manage the household and the kids when emotions are calm and balanced. Do you feel this way? How much better could life be if you rocked your body or your mind?

TIP: Make use of humor. You can say the same thing to your partner with a smile and a twinkle in your eye and it will be much better received (and you might even be able to avoid having dishware hurled at your head).

You might be thinking, "But health is a personal thing. Why do I have to share this with my partner?" By virtue of being in a relationship, your lives are intertwined. Here are a couple of examples: You probably eat meals together. If one person is going to make a significant change in the way they eat, this will be much more easily accomplished with the support of the other person, who may be preparing meals, eating with you, or selecting restaurants when you go out. Or maybe the issue is scheduling medical appointments that can take you away from the family, and your partner will be more supportive of your absence if they know the bigger goals behind your absence. Besides, what cannot be done better together than apart?

Obviously health includes many things, and we could write pages and pages here. But we got bored even thinking about it! Visit the website (have we said it too many times yet?) www.48HourRetreat.com and you will find all kinds of checklists and tips for your health, if you are so inclined.

OUR STORY: Hey, NBC! We Want Our Royalties

We keep checking our mailbox every day for a check from NBC. We think we had the idea for *The Biggest Loser* long before it was ever on TV. At least that was what came out of our retreat one year. Both of us determined that we wanted to be healthier (okay, let's be honest, we just wanted to drop some pounds and look better in our clothes). And we are competitive people (we even bet on the number of previews at a movie). So we decided to motivate each other. We started a ten-week contest to see who could lose the highest percentage of weight.

Every Friday morning we weighed in and wrote our weights on a chart — and it worked for both of us. When Amanda weighed in and saw Richard was a little ahead, she would redouble her efforts and do a few more minutes of cardio each day the following week. And if Amanda surged, Richard would stop himself from grabbing that extra snack at night. In the end, Richard ended up half a percentage point ahead of Amanda (Amanda was really just one good poop away from winning), so we called it a tie and we both enjoyed the prize (a weekend away).

THE SHORT AND SNAPPY SUMMARY OF OUR BRILLIANT DISCUSSION POINTS:

- How do you feel about your current health status?

- How does your current health condition affect your everyday life?

- Are there specific areas in your life that would be better if your overall health were to improve?

- Don't forget to apply THE METHOD — most people have a lot of BIG DREAMS and action plans they can find in this area.

CHAPTER 17
HOME

(Our House...Is a Very, Very, Very Fine House)

CHAPTER 17
HOME
(Our House...Is a Very, Very, Very Fine House)

"A house is not a home unless it contains food and fire for the mind as well as the body."
— Benjamin Franklin

OUR STORY: Tiptoeing into the Shallow End or Diving into the Deep (Amanda's Take)

When Richard and I bought our current home, part of the reason we knew it was the right house for us was because it has a big flat backyard. I wanted to have an in-ground pool, and the lot just seemed to beg to have a big hole dug right in the middle of it. For a couple of years after we moved in I would say things like "...and the pool" and Richard would be like, "Yeah, yeah, right...the pool." And again it would come back up and I'd reiterate "...and the pool" and he'd look at me like I was crazy.

Then one day I said, "The pool is going on our retreat agenda because I don't see it in my backyard yet and I don't know why I don't see it in my backyard yet." And Richard said, "I don't know where you think a pool is coming from. We don't have the money for a pool." And I said, "Hogwash we don't have the money for a pool." (Richard's editorial note: who really says *hogwash*? Amanda cursed, and she just doesn't want to admit it in writing.) "What are you talking about? We make things happen that we want to have happen.

continued

You're just blocking the pool because you don't find it important. Clearly this is a crock. You don't think my thing is important, so it's not happening." Richard said that wasn't true and it wasn't fair.

So we took our retreat time, some of our actual retreat time, and we went to a local pool place, and yeah, I was completely living in some kind of drug-induced haze apparently, because the kind of pool I wanted starts, minimum, in our area, at thirty to forty thousand dollars. Probably what I was looking at would run far more than that.

I was mad that Richard wasn't supporting my dream, but the reality was my dream just was not realistic, and once we actually sat down at our retreat and did the work and I found out really what it would cost, I realized, "Oh, no, we can't have a pool," and Richard said, "Right, that's what I've been telling you."

So nobody was wrong, but real resentments grew because I thought Richard was ignoring what I really wanted. But in reality that perception was just not accurate. It could have gone on forever and it could have blown up into much bigger issues, and in my head I would have been saying, "He just doesn't love me enough; why are we spending money on other things when we could be saving for my dream?"

Doing the work of clarifying the reality of the pool situation diffused all of that and avoided what could have become a big issue of resentment in our marriage.

The word *home* has a lot of different meanings, and it can evoke many different emotions as well. For some people the American Dream of owning your own place is what brought them to this country in the first place. For others, recent economic conditions might have you viewing your home as an albatross around your neck. No matter your current condition, the ideal for most of us is to have our home be our sanctuary — a home base where we reconnect with each other and recharge our batteries, and a place where we can seek refuge from the big, mean, ugly forces of the world that conspire against us. Maybe even a refuge with a Man Cave!!!

Whether you are renting or you own, live in a high-rise building or in the country, your home is important!

NOTE: Much of this chapter has to do with owning your own house or condo. If you are renting right now, much of this chapter might not fully apply to you. Feel free to skim the chapter and decide what you want to discuss and what you want to skip. Or maybe you want to use this time to discuss whether you want to continue to rent where you are now or perhaps make a move.

SELF-ANALYSIS

Take a critical look at your home and see what is or isn't working for you. This should include not only the physical building (there could be financial, maintenance, or decor issues that you need to address), but also the systems in place that help you run your home. While you are looking at the various parts of your home, also look to yourself and reflect about what your home means to you and what makes you happiest in your home. Try to determine the relationships you have between your feelings and the actions you take in your home.

What is your mental picture of your ideal home? Write a few paragraphs about your home. Focus not only on the physical building, but also on how you feel when you are in your home — the atmosphere, the mood that is created (or you would like to be created), and whether your home is clean and crisp or feels warm and lived in. What is your favorite room (or what would you like your favorite room to be if you could make it just the way you want it to be)?

Is there a move in your future? According to Wiki.Answers.com, 75 percent of the people in the United States move an average of once every five years. This probably means that there is a move sometime in your future. Now is the time to start discussing some of the issues surrounding moving. If you are going to move, would you buy or rent? What type of a home would you like to live in? How long do you anticipate you will be in your next home? What items are important for you and for your partner? Each of you should draw up a list of wants and needs in regard to a new home.

How is your village? Hillary Clinton famously noted that "it takes a village." Amanda also has a very good friend, Melody, who for years encouraged us to move out of the *house* we owned and move our family into a *neighborhood* where we knew our neighbors and had a real sense of community. We never put much stock in what either of these women was trying to tell us until we actually moved into a village. Now we look back on the years that we merely lived in a house and wonder how we made it through life without the love, support, and good times that the people in our neighborhood provide to us.

Take stock of your neighborhood. Do you live in a village? If you only live in a house (condo, apartment), what can you do to create that sense of community? These types of connections can be so important at any stage in life, whether it is neighbors you can carpool with and swap children's sleepovers with, friends you can vacation with in your empty nest years, or people who can check in on you in your golden years.

Are you beautiful on the inside and out? Now focus on your current home. Are you happy with the state of your home? Talk about any issues you might have.

Cleanliness: Though it sounds trivial, household chores are a major source of conflict for many couples, not always because of the actual tasks, but often because of their perceived meaning.

"Rows about housework are often about unfilled needs for respect and worth," says relationship psychotherapist Paula Hall in an article for www.SixWise.com. Indeed, if one partner feels they are putting in more effort around the house than the other, it brings up notions that the other person does not respect them enough to help out. It also brings up issues of power, especially if the person making more money feels they shouldn't have to pitch in around the home.

"Love and respect are essential ingredients in a relationship and sometimes housework becomes the battleground where you fight for these needs. Housework can become a distraction from the main issue," says Hall.

Further adding to the potential conflict is that everyone has different opinions about what a clean home is. If one partner is a neat freak and the other is more laid back, it can lead to a constant struggle. Consider how each of you feels about the subject and where you can make changes or put systems into place to help achieve balance.

Decor: Do you have the same priorities? What would you like to see changed or upgraded in the next year? Put together a plan to make your home as you would like it.

Outside: If you have a yard or your property is landscaped, is everything in good order? Are you pleased with the way you use the space? If not, take time to put plans in place for sprucing up the place.

Regular check-ups aren't just for the Doc — Do you do regular maintenance on your home, or do you only think of your home when a problem occurs? Doing regular maintenance not only heads off disasters, but can help save money by keeping your systems working at peak performance. Develop your plan of attack and schedule for regular home maintenance.

SOLUTION CENTER: Divide up the duties — which items are best handled by each partner and when you plan to have each of the tasks completed. The list can seem overwhelming, but once you get in the swing of it, it will seem like second nature. Perhaps you can set aside one day each month that can be your day to take care of all of your household projects — the maintenance and then any other tasks you would like to do. It is often much easier if both people are working at the same time...sort of the misery loves company theory. Be sure to plan a nice evening when you are done so you can celebrate all of your hard work. If doing the tasks yourself is out of your expertise, contact a handyman service about setting up a regular maintenance schedule.

THE SHORT AND SNAPPY SUMMARY OF OUR BRILLIANT DISCUSSION POINTS:

- What do you really want/need in a home?

- Is a move in your future?

- How's your "village"?

- How are things on the inside of your home?

- How about the outside?

- Do you have a regular maintenance plan for your home?

- Have you applied The Method to this section?

CHAPTER 18
FAMILY
(We Are Fam-i-ly)

CHAPTER 18
FAMILY
(We Are Fam-i-ly)

"If you cannot get rid of the family skeleton, you may as well make it dance."
— George Bernard Shaw, *Immaturity*

OUR STORY: And They Said It Couldn't Be Done! (Richard's Take)

Because of our personal circumstances, we needed to create more action plans than most people when it came to having children.

Before I met Amanda she had cancer, and as a result she couldn't carry babies. We ended up having our son through a surrogate, and we adopted our daughter from Russia, so that became an obvious topic of conversation at our retreats for several years.

First it was planning about whether it was time to have a child, then about how it was going to happen, then about how we were going to pay for it. Another time it was "should we bag the surrogacy route for child #2 and go with the adoption route?" Those were big, big goals and we worked through a lot of it— not everything, but a lot of it — on our retreats. We'd set milestones for the next year and put plans in place to reach them. In fact, we found *where* to find a surrogate at a retreat. (Ends up you really can find everything on the internet.)

continued

Sometimes portions of our retreats are real working sessions where we have an issue and we sit down and get out the computers and do the research. It's not all talking all the time, and this is one of those things it would be hard for one partner to do without getting input from the other! It's so much easier at a retreat because we have the time. It's not after work on Friday when we're tired...no, we're here, let's get it done. And we did. And we have two beautiful (though rarely perfect) children as a result of the work that we started at our retreats.

When many of us think of family we think of the traditional nuclear family unit — two parents and kids. But in today's world that definition of family is changing. And in the context of this retreat you might consider a much broader or different notion of family. Because there are so many issues to consider here, we'll break this down into various stages-of-life sections. Obviously choose the one that applies to you and dive into an exploration of your situation.

SELF-ANALYSIS

How can you and your partner form a stronger team in dealing with your children and/or aging family members? Are there areas in which you feel you aren't giving your best effort as a parent? Why? What can you change, and what is necessary to make that happen?

If you were to make changes in the way you parent your children, what effects can you anticipate these changes would have on your life, your family, and your relationship? Maybe you haven't considered the effects that the knock-down drag-out fights you have with your son have on the rest of the family. Or maybe you don't see the stress that the fights with your daughter put on her siblings. Seeing how changes in one area will positively affect others might give you the motivation to make changes for the better.

The expansion phase — Do you wish to hear the pitter-patter of little feet? Are those two or four feet? Either way, both children and pets require a big commitment (yes, in some ways we are equating a baby and a puppy — just roll with it, okay?!?). Before you commit to either one, look at your schedule and your lifestyle. Assess what your true desires are and how you will split up the workload if you have an addition to the family. Talk about your timeline for adding a family member and how the process might go. Write out your expectations for how this change will affect your relationship and household. What will be better? What will be worse? How will you deal with the additional responsibilities? What about the changes in your schedule and your free time? Take the time to let each person voice their feelings on the subject and admit honestly how much effort they are willing to put in.

Obviously, at least to every parent reading this, you can't plan for every eventuality that parenthood brings. But we think it's helpful to do some thinking about it before you jump in.

The care and feeding of the little monsters — Someone should really come up with a manual for children. Or maybe a license should be required for procreation. Because really, this is often the most difficult job that we do for which we have no training. So it is no surprise that this section is in the book. In addition to the fact that childrearing is a challenging effort, it is also a significant issue that couples fight about. And the source of that dissention is often the fact that you have differing viewpoints about how to best support your children. So take this time and talk about your kids. Break it down into small parts and see where you can find consensus and where you need to compromise.

- The basic approach — Do you both approach parenting the same way? If you don't, take time to appreciate the benefits of your children seeing different "management" styles in action. If you do, celebrate the ease of your singular focus. Either way, do an assessment of your approach and make sure that you are doing the best you can for your child/children.

- Parenting plan — Our good friend Shannan develops a parenting plan for each of her children. She looks at the next year and identifies the milestones that they are likely to encounter and determines how she wants to approach them. She finds the lessons she wants to teach them and looks for opportunities to work that information into their lives naturally. This kind of forethought makes her parenting very intentional and yet very natural at the same time. Because she has thought out the things she might want to say, she is prepared when the opportunities for discussion present themselves and doesn't shy away from difficult discussions. (BTW, we don't do this! At all. Maybe one day we'll do the same thing, but until then Shannan gets the extra parent points.)

- Assess each child and their current strengths and weaknesses. What do you need to do in the following year to better help them develop? Are there special skills that need to be developed or do you need to intervene on their behalf at school? Are there additional athletic or extracurricular activities (dance, scouts, music, etc.) that you feel are important?

SOLUTION CENTER: Remember those "Venting Cards" we talked about in the Ground Rules chapter? Well, the same concept can apply to your children as well. As parents we typically want to fix things for our kids so that we can make their lives happy and pain-free. But sometimes we just can't seem to locate that magic wand. But that is okay. Often what our kids really need is someone to listen to them and sympathize with them rather than jumping in to provide solutions.

We have developed a special set of "Venting Cards" for you to use when your kids just want to get something off of their chest — you can get your very own set on our website.

Grown, but not gone? Ahhh...the curse of the economy. When we graduated from college it was pretty much expected that you would go out and get a job and live on your own. (Richard is pretty sure his parents changed the locks on all the doors when he went away to college.) But these days the economics are not quite the same. Many parents are faced with their little birdies returning to their nest. This is not a subject we have had to deal with yet, but maybe someday we will. In the meantime, we gathered input from our friends and here is what they said you should talk about when you are faced with these issues:

- If your adult children are living in your home, do you both have the same perspective about that (is it okay with both of you)? If not, can you find a plan that you can both agree on that makes it more okay for each of you?

- Is there an exit strategy for your child/children? Obviously the goal for most adults is to be self-sufficient and live a fully realized life. While we certainly understand wanting to help your children get established, if there is no plan to move on, you often get mired in complacency. Use the retreat as motivation to develop a plan for growth and movement toward the future with your child/children. (Perhaps part of that is helping them identify their own goals and dreams.)

Beyond your immediate branches — As we age, our parents age too (duh!). At some point we can find our role switching from child to caregiver. This is often a difficult transition that can put a lot of stress on a relationship. Whether you are in the throes of dealing with this kind of situation or you see it looming on your horizon like an impending tornado, now is the time to discuss plans and implications.

- What is the current health of your family members? Can you anticipate what kind of care might be needed and when? Do you have a plan for how that care will be provided?

- What are the financial implications for your family? Do your family members have their finances in order? Do they have long-term care plans and insurance? Will you be called upon to contribute financially to their care?

- If one of your family members becomes unable to care for themselves, what are their wishes for care? Do they want to stay in their own home and have care come to them? Would they prefer to move to a care facility or assisted living? Would you prefer to have them move in with you?

- Do you have siblings? If so, how will care and costs be shared among everyone involved?

In addition to resolving these issues within your relationship, use your retreat as a springboard for discussing these issues with your family members. Schedule a time to talk with your parents, aunts, etc. to fully understand what their wishes are for their aging years. That meeting is also a good time to make sure all of their affairs are in order and that you know where important papers are kept and how to access information in case of emergency. Be sure to include other family members (siblings) in the conversation so you are all on the same page. This will help avoid disagreements about care at a later date.

We know you're rolling your eyes at us! We hate this, too, especially Amanda. But we had the awkward discussions and are better for it.

Divorce — dealing with the others in your life (NOTE: This question is for dealing with a previous divorce, not for planning your own!) — This is not a subject with which we have personal experience. We are very thankful that we have kept it together for all these years, but we have friends who had different outcomes in their relationships. So we interviewed REAL PEOPLE...not "experts" or therapists, or anyone like that. After talking with many people in many different situations, we realized that there are several key items to be discussed that form the foundation for success in dealing with exes in the context of your current relationship.

- How does the status of your previous relationship affect your current relationship? Each person should think about that and then share their *honest* assessment with each other. If there are ugly leftover feelings, now is the time to talk them out. And remember that you should say how you honestly feel, and if you are on the listening end you should believe your partner and let any preconceived notions go.

- How is your communication with your ex? Do you have open and good lines of communication? If not, this *might* be the time to work toward establishing a more open line of communication. As you might have gleaned in the book thus far, we are big believers in honest communication. If you hope that your current relationship will be successful, having as little discord as possible from your past relationships only makes sense.

- Can you seek to find balance? This could really apply to the whole book, but in particular when you are managing multiple relationships and there are many people involved, can you find a place where all people involved feel like their interests are represented and they are getting their fair share of their needs met?

- Have boundaries been established, and are they clear and maintained? When children are moving between different households and families, each family should be clear about expectations and boundaries. Each family should set up their rules and share them with each other so that the expectations and consequences are clear.

- Are you clear about the financial expectations and implications? Usually there are court rulings in place that outline these requirements, but make sure that your partner understands not only what is *required* of you pertaining to your children, but also what you WANT to do (for instance, you only *have* to pay for child support, but you might *want* to pay for their senior trip abroad).

- Is there such a thing as too much love? We would say no. Our friend Malinda reminded us that in blended families it just means that there are "more people to love the children." If you can focus on that end of the relationship and check any jealousy or other negative feelings at the door, then everyone can be happier.

We hope you have good conversations in this area. But you *know* that it can't stop with just the two of you. You really should involve *all* of the people in your relationship. Your kids, your ex. Plan to have discussions with them to share the results of your retreat. (You might even share this book with the adults so they know where you are coming from…maybe they will even have their own retreat and be all the happier for it.)

OUR STORY: Call In the Cavalry…We Need Back-Up (Amanda's Take)

Here's a small issue that could have blown up into a huge deal or simmered at a low angry boil underneath the surface. It's an example of a small thing in a marriage that when tweaked makes a big difference, and it shows that a retreat is not all about the really big life-shattering discussions, but sometimes it's the small things that make a huge difference.

This issue was about getting babysitters. We get babysitters a lot. We enjoy our friends and we enjoy time for just the two of us so we can be together.

It used to be my responsibility to arrange for babysitters, and for some reason I really resented it. I resented the fact that I did all these other things around the house and when we were going out I had to take care of that, too. I held on to that resentment for who knows how many years — it really started building up.

continued

In fact, I started to dread going out (or at least the process of getting ready) because I would have to deal with the sitter. I'd have to find one and if that one cancelled I'd handle that responsibility. The whole process put a pall on our special evenings out.

So one year at our retreat we were discussing the subject of the kids and sitters came up. I guess I must have visibly flinched because Richard asked what was wrong. I hesitated, but he prodded (gently), and when we got down to the heart of the fact that I was ticked off because I was getting the sitter all the time, he said, "I can do that…you just needed to tell me that you didn't like doing that."

So now Richard handles getting all our sitters. And now he ends up being the one who gets the kids their dinner and greets the sitter when they get here and gives them the rundown for the evening. What it does for me is:

1. I'm no longer a bear about the whole sitter burden so it changed that dynamic between the two of us on nights when we are going out.

2. I'm in a good mood when we're leaving the house because I've already made the transition from Mom to Date Wife. That is a benefit for both of us.

3. I feel more equality and sharing of the workload.

So that conversation that we had at a retreat about babysitters, which is such a small thing, had great benefits for our relationship.

Everybody thinks that something monumental has to happen at a retreat. Sometimes it's "smallumental" — really a little thing that has all these other beneficial consequences.

THE SHORT AND SNAPPY SUMMARY OF OUR BRILLIANT DISCUSSION POINTS:

- How can you form a stronger partnership in dealing with your family?

- What effects would changes have on the other members of your family?

- How will you deal with your particular situation?
    - The expansion phase
    - The care and feeding of the little monsters
    - Grown, but not gone?
    - Beyond your immediate branches
    - Divorce — dealing with the others in your life

- There can be actions plans to support BIG DREAMS in this area, too, so don't forget to apply THE METHOD.

CHAPTER 19
SCHEDULING

(I'm Late, I'm Late...
For a Very Important Date)

CHAPTER 19
SCHEDULING
(I'm Late, I'm Late…for a Very Important Date)

"Happiness [is] only real when shared."
— Jon Krakauer

OUR STORY: We Really Can't Keep Meeting this Way…Or Should We?!? (Richard's Take)

One outcome from our retreat that has made a big impact is setting up family "systems."

We've developed, over the years, systems that are automatic now and make life so much easier. We have a Sunday night meeting, and it's very much like any meeting you would have at work — we have an agenda and we have assignments. If we need to discuss something new, somebody is responsible for it and comes prepared; just like you wouldn't call a business meeting and just say, "Hey guys, we're having a meeting." We know what we're going to talk about and we come prepared. If we're not prepared, then we say, "Can I have five or ten minutes?" or we say, "You know what, we need to talk about that one particular item later."

At our Sunday meetings we review the calendar for the next ten days, decide who's taking kids where, figure out who's making dinner, etc.

The difference in my week from when we have a meeting versus when we somehow get sidetracked and miss the meeting is significant. If we don't have a meeting, I spend all week going,

continued

"What is on the schedule tonight?" and "Who's cooking dinner tonight? Is it you or is it me?"

That's one thing that grew out of our retreats — weekly meetings. And we wouldn't want to do without them — even my "free spirit" wife!

Recently Richard said that he wanted to "simplify life." After Amanda got done laughing at the mere mention of those words, she asked what he meant. He responded that we were just too busy, being pulled in too many directions, and because of that we were always stressed and we weren't enjoying life. While we couldn't really disagree, the concept of cutting things out of our schedule seemed impossible. I mean, we have a reputation to uphold — we are the "we never turn down an invitation" people. And then there are our children; what are they going to cut out? Do we have to make a choice between sports and scouts?!?! Who is going to tell them they can't do the things they love?

It was only after deep inspection of the things we put on our schedule that we could identify those items that actually feed our souls and those that are energy-sappers.

The harsh reality is that there are a finite number of hours in a day. And in today's world there are ever-growing demands on time. Scrutinize how you spend your time in order to cut out the crap that is nonproductive and make room for the things that make you happier and bring you closer to being the people and family that you want to be.

SELF-ANALYSIS

How are your friendships? According to a December 2008 study published in the British Medical Journal, scientists from Harvard

University and UC San Diego showed that happiness spreads readily through social networks of family members, friends, and neighbors. Knowing someone who is happy makes you 15.3 percent more likely to be happy yourself, the study found. A happy friend of a friend increases your odds of happiness by 9.8 percent. And even your neighbor's sister's happy friend can give you a 5.6 percent boost.

According to the Everyday Health website, spending time with friends has long-term physical and emotional benefits:

1. Socially engaged adults age more successfully.

2. Friends can help you achieve your weight and fitness goals.

3. Happy friends spread the happiness.

4. Having a circle of friends or being a leader in a group brings happiness.

5. Friends lessen grief.

6. Being social boosts your immune system. (More positive emotions boost immunity.)

Do you each see enough of your friends? A support group is critical to the success of a marriage. Each person should maintain their own friendships with people they share interests with. Now is the time to make a plan to keep in touch with these people. Maybe it is identifying one night a week that is "friend night" when you each go your separate ways and see friends. Or maybe it is an effort to write and send cards to friends.

Also consider couples with whom you maintain relationships. Have you seen enough of those couples? Should you put more effort into seeing those friends? Conversely, do you maintain friendships out of obligation when they aren't adding anything positive to your lives?

Our friends who know we do our retreat each year also know that we review our friendships. They have been known to bring us bribes or write us poems to secure their space in our lives for another year (we have a fun group of friends with a great sense of humor). Some years we have decided to let a friendship just fade away, and twice now we actively eliminated toxic relationships from our lives.

We heard recently that people become like the six people they spend the most time with. Who are the six people you spend your time with? Are they people you want to be like? Perhaps you are becoming like them whether you are actively choosing to or not. Cut the bad and keep the good!

WORD OF CAUTION: Remember where your alliances are at all times. You should be careful about sharing information that your partner has told you in confidence. Also be cautious of relationships with members of the opposite sex. While we never would rule out such relationships, be sure that your partner feels comfortable with your role in one of these relationships, and always maintain appropriate boundaries.

What kind of exciting events are in your future? Are there favorite events you participate in on an annual basis? Are there things you would like to do but have never been able to do? Brainstorm right now and come up with a list of things. You can always do research later to see when the events are occurring. How about vacations? Do you have the same ideas? What about trying something new? Often people find themselves with nothing to do just because they didn't plan. Take the time now to plan for your future fun. It will not only make your scheduling easier, but it will give you and your family something to look forward to.

It's the most stressful time of the year — Many people report feeling very anxious or even depressed around major holidays. The cause is often attributed to family dynamics. Take time to discuss holidays and major family celebrations (like birthdays, anniversaries, etc.) with your partner. Do you share time between the different sides of your family? Does everyone get together? What are the current (or potential) sources of conflict, and what can you do to anticipate and minimize them? If holidays are a source of trouble in your relationship, visit our website and download the holiday worksheet to help guide you through the discussion.

What does your calendar look like next week? Does your life look like a train about to careen off the tracks? Do you live by your calendar? Are you always late for appointments? Do you bake cookies at midnight the night before the school bake sale? Take a look at your family schedule and see how you can streamline things. Are things working for you? And don't be so excited if your calendar is empty next week...this might indicate that you are trying to keep too much in your head and you are suffering from a lack of organization.

What is your BIG DREAM for this area of your life? How could your life be richer if you enhanced your friendships and filled your calendar with "want tos" instead of "have tos"? Make your plans around the dreams that you want to see come true and watch the wonderful gifts that unfold around you.

THE SHORT AND SNAPPY SUMMARY OF OUR BRILLIANT DISCUSSION POINTS:

- How are your friendships, and are you really nurturing them?
- What kind of exciting events are in your future?
- Can you do more advance planning for the most stressful times of the year?
- What does your calendar look like next week?
- What are your BIG DREAMS for this area of your life?

OUR STORY: We'd Like to Renegotiate Our Contract, Please!

We told you our friends are funny…and here is an example. This is a Top 10 list that was presented to us before we went on our retreat one year. (These friends were watching our kids for the weekend while we went away.)

Top 10 Reasons the Barneys Should Remain Friends with Barb and Dave:

10. They watch your kids so you can have sex…well, okay …sleep late.

9. Dave makes really great cocktails.

8. They balance out the spectrum with your so-called "millionaire player" friends.

7. They are charming, witty, and laugh at your jokes even when they are not funny…and they very often are not.

6. They continually pray for you so you don't end up in…

5. When you mess up you can say, "Well, at least we are not Barb and Dave."

4. Dave has no shame when it comes to providing quality entertainment.

3. They can laugh at themselves, each other, and more importantly…you.

2. They love your kids like they are their own.

1. They are the people you could call at three a.m. when you wake up in jail.

CHAPTER 20
INTIMACY
(We're Bringing Sexy Back)

CHAPTER 20
INTIMACY
(We're Bringing Sexy Back)

"Sex is emotion in motion."
— Mae West
"Some things are better than sex, and some are worse,
but there's nothing exactly like it."
— W.C. Fields

If there is one part of life that is guaranteed to change from year to year, but that perhaps we don't think will change, it is sex! There, we said it. This is going to be a whole chapter about sex. But before you get all excited thinking this is a mini-version of *50 Shades of Grey*, let us set an appropriate expectation. In this section you might not end up talking about new positions or different ways to spice up your sex life. What you are going to talk about is things you might do to maintain or increase the level of sexual satisfaction in your relationship (but who knows, that might end up being new positions or different ways to spice up your sex life).

Unfortunately the last thing most couples actually *talk* about is their sex life. Not that we don't hear about it. We are bombarded by sex every day — on TV, in advertising, in magazines, on billboards, even on buses. And often we hear that couples are having sex like bunnies, and we wonder why our relationship is just not matching up. Well, if you are anything like us, we are just not able to read minds, and we're guessing that you are not much good at it either. So now is the time to sit down with your partner and have an honest discussion. Yes, it might be awkward. So what! It's good for you.

Use this agenda as an excuse if you have to. If you are having trouble finding the words to say, we have a great book for you — *365 Questions for Couples* by Michael J. Beck and Stanis Marusak Beck. Make a promise to each other that you will answer any questions asked honestly. Another ground rule is that if you ask a question, you must also answer the same question.

SELF-ANALYSIS

Are your needs being met in the bedroom? Do you believe your partner's needs are being met in the bedroom? Many of us have baggage from the way we were raised. We were given messages about what kind of sexual creatures we should be. Now is the time to look deep into yourself to determine what *you* want, and how you want your sex life to be.

Is the sex you have good for both of you? Do you want your partner to do something they aren't currently doing? This part of the discussion might end up being very technical. You should talk about things you like and don't like. When it comes to your physical experiences, there can often be a lot of ego tied up in sex, so try to listen objectively to what your partner is telling you. Remember that if they enjoy the experience, you are more likely to have a great time as well.

According to *your* standards (not those of media or anyone else you know), are you having sex often enough? If we listen to the media we can quickly become convinced that our sex life sucks. According to one survey or the latest nighttime drama, it seems that happy couples are having sex all the time. But you know what? Who cares! It doesn't matter what other people are doing, it matters what you (and your partner) want to do. The trick here is trying to find a frequency that meets both of your needs. Be creative. Find compromise. Work toward solutions for everyone.

Do you feel intimately connected to your partner? Really being honest about intimacy is difficult. It is certainly a topic that can be dangerous. But that doesn't mean you should avoid it; it just means that you should approach this discussion honestly, but with caring.

Do you have any sexual fantasies that you have never shared with your partner? (Sharing them doesn't mean you have to act on them, but talking about them may open up doors to further discussion and learning what interests your partner.) We have found that we can have some fun here, even if we have no intention of acting on our fantasies. Sharing them in a non-judgmental forum and understanding how and why our partner thinks or feels a certain way can be very enlightening. And it might lead to some new excitement. (NOTE: Make sure that ceiling is reinforced before you install that love swing.)

What are five things your spouse could do (*outside* of the bedroom) that would get you in the mood? Did you know that the biggest sexual organ is actually the brain? That's right. Eighty-five percent of sex is in the brain, and for most people sex begins well before they take off their clothes and jump into bed (especially for women).

Women often expect our men to be mind readers. And we think that unless they do things without us asking, then the gesture just isn't "real." Well, that is just a big pile of fecal matter! Unless we women have developed the ability to remember every box score and know the lines to all our guys' favorite movies, then we can't expect them to know what little things they can do that will make our day. On the flip side, a majority of men prefer action over items and appreciate nice gestures over gifts. So let's help each other out. Tell your partner what makes you happy, and then take it as a sign of their affection when they *do* these things for you.

OUR STORY: I'm Bringing Sexy Back (Amanda's Take)

Sometimes the transformations from a retreat aren't seen at the end of the retreat, and sometimes they aren't even seen for months. And sometimes the transformations don't happen as a result of the conversations you have, but rather the conversations you are too afraid to have. This is a story about exactly that.

In 2007 we had our retreat as usual. As best I can recall there was nothing really unusual about it. It was *fine*. *Just* fine. Not awful, but certainly nothing great. But if I have to be honest there was a big issue that was weighing on me but that I just couldn't bring myself to bring up. It was our sex life. For me it wasn't good enough. We didn't have sex very often, and when we did it seemed very rote. I was pretty sure it was just me thinking that and I didn't want to hurt Richard's feelings and his ego by bringing it up. So we went through the intimacy questions at our retreat and I gave pat answers, and so did Richard. Everything was *fine*.

As I lamented to my wonderful friend Shannan *after* our retreat that I had missed the opportunity to discuss the issue, I explained I didn't say anything because I didn't know what to say. And she encouraged me to think about the right words so that if the time ever presented itself I would be ready.

continued

A few weeks later I worked up the courage and the words did come to me. And I was completely shocked when I said I thought our sex life was stale, and Richard agreed! He felt the same way. Not only did he agree, but he had a solution. He was due for a trip with some buddies, and instead he suggested we get away…to somewhere warm and romantic. Within three weeks we were jetting off to a tropical paradise.

Now I know you don't want all the gory details of the trip, but let's just say that it reignited a flame and probably changed the course of our marriage.

I don't want you to think that it was the trip that heated things up, because in reality it was the fact that we brought the issues out into the light. And we started to talk it through and problem-solve around it until we came up with some solutions *together*.

THE SHORT AND SNAPPY SUMMARY OF OUR BRILLIANT DISCUSSION POINTS:

- Are your needs being met in the bedroom?

- Is the sex you have good for both of you?

- According to *your* standards (not those of media or anyone else you know), are you having sex often enough?

- Do you feel intimately connected to your partner?

- Do you have any sexual fantasies that you have never shared with your partner?

- What are five things your spouse could do (*outside* of the bedroom) that would get you in the mood?

- Don't let the good conversations to go waste; be sure to identify some BIG DREAMS and create those action steps!

CHAPTER 21
YOUR TOPIC HERE
(That's Right –
You're the Expert)

CHAPTER 21
YOUR TOPIC HERE
(That's Right — You're the Expert)

"In essence, if we want to direct our lives, we must take control of our consistent actions. It's not what we do once in a while that shapes our lives, but what we do consistently. "
— Tony Robbins

All along we have told you that this is YOUR retreat; that we are suggesting topics for you to discuss, but that you should be adjusting the agenda to suit your own needs and situations. This chapter is the placeholder for any items that you want to discuss that didn't fit neatly into one of the previous topics we have outlined.

In creating your own topic(s), just follow a few simple steps:

1. Identify the questions that you will both use in your self-analysis phase.

2. Write them down (so you know you are both talking about the same topic).

3. Apply THE METHOD to the questions you have developed.

4. Visit our website and tell us what you added — it might benefit others as well!

THE SHORT AND SNAPPY SUMMARY OF *YOUR* BRILLIANT DISCUSSION POINTS:

- [Your first discussion point here]

- We're sure you came up with some good ones.

- They had better not be better than ours!

- How many questions did you have already?

CHAPTER 22
BUDGET REVIEW
(Please Stop the Pain!)

CHAPTER 22
BUDGET REVIEW
(Please Stop the Pain!)

"A budget tells us what we can't afford, but it doesn't keep us from buying it."
— William Feather

BUDGET REVIEW

We know what you are saying — "You gotta be kidding me, more money talk?" That's right. We warned you this would be here, and now the time has arrived.

The good news is that this discussion is all about possibilities. You have spent your time during this retreat thinking about your joint goals, your desires, and your dreams. Now is when you get to work out the financial plan that will make those dreams a reality.

The other good news is that action is much quicker and less tearful than no action — at least for Amanda!

You've hopefully spent an energizing weekend coming up with a veritable cornucopia of exciting opportunities; a plethora of possibilities; great gobs of grand ideas; a bushel full of...Okay! Okay! How about: "many plans." Anyhow, some of those plans might require a financial commitment. As you wrap up the retreat, it's time to figure out what your finances allow and/or what changes you both want to make in order to reach your goals.

Hopefully you have kept a list of any budget-related items. (If not, take time now and go back and review your action items and their financial implications.) Review your household budget in light of the decisions you made this weekend. Do you need to save for a new home, schooling, or an addition to the family? Make the necessary adjustments in your budget to assist you in meeting your goals on your timeline.

You might not get everything sorted out but you should have taken your list of goals and decided how to approach them financially.

One word of caution — As with many of the other items you discussed this weekend, financial decisions cannot be made in a vacuum. There are only two ways to make a positive change in your financial picture — either cut down on expenses or increase your income. Often these changes have costs that are more than you want to bear (like increased work hours resulting in time away from your family).

SOLUTION CENTER: If, after consideration and discussion, you agree that you would like to make some financial changes in your life, you might want to consider some of these suggestions:

Get a job — If you don't already have a job, now would be the time to find one. And if you already have one job, is there a possibility to get a second job?

Other streams of revenue — Find other ways to put money into your bank account. See where there are opportunities to make additional money doing things you love or doing things you already do. It could be something as simple as doing errands for a neighbor who needs help, or watching a child after school. Perhaps you like to tinker on cars and your neighbor routinely takes his car to the shop; see if you can become his "personal mechanic." Or hang out your shingle and become a "consultant."

continued

A free lunch — Okay, rarely is there such a thing as a free lunch, but taking your lunch to work can save significant money over the long haul. It really isn't hard once you get in the habit. Simply double the recipe when you are making dinner, and you'll have enough extra for several meals during the week. Other things like cutting out your daily trip to Starbucks or that bagel in the morning can really add up over time. And to force yourself to save the money, put the amount you would have spent each day into an envelope and deposit it in the bank at the end of the week.

Location, location, location — This is radical, but perhaps your goals are radical, too! If you want to make lifestyle changes that require significant financial resources (like a career change that comes with a major pay cut), you might want to consider downsizing your home. In doing so you might realize a cash gain from the sale. You might also wish to relocate to a home that is closer to public transportation or closer to your new job (therefore saving more money in transportation costs).

Whatever your goals, don't immediately settle for "can't be done." Take some time to look for all the creative ways you might be able to accomplish your BIG DREAMS.

SECTION 4
Making It Stick

CHAPTER 23
MAKING PLANS
(Time for Action, Jackson)

CHAPTER 23
MAKING PLANS
(Time for Action, Jackson)

"A goal without a plan is just a wish."
— Antoine de Saint-Exupery

Congratulations! You made it through the weekend. We are sure you experienced joys and revelations, but perhaps you had some rough spots as well. You deserve credit for doing the work necessary to build a strong foundation for yourselves, your relationship, and your family.

Improving your relationship is not a one-shot deal. As we continue to grow and change with age, our relationships need to evolve. The work you did in this retreat will be strengthened if you continue to monitor your relationship and the progress it is making. It's helpful if you keep the work you did in a central notebook. This way you will be able to find your notes and track your progress.

We recommend that you hold a full-blown retreat every year at roughly the same time, and that you hold a mini-retreat at the halfway point. At the mini-retreat you can reexamine your goals and major touchstone issues to see if you are on track, and correct any small issues before they become large issues.

Here's the key: The progress you made this weekend will be lost unless you put your thoughts and plans into action. Surely there were questions left unanswered — maybe you needed more information; maybe you just needed to think about things for a while. Before you let the energy of the weekend fade away, make plans to stay on the right track.

Follow-up work — While most of us would love to take 48 hours and then declare everything is great with our lives, it just doesn't work that way. At the end of this weekend you'll know much more about each other and you have plans for the future. You also have a to-do list. Hopefully as the weekend went along, you kept a list of action items for the following weeks. These might include starting a new eating/exercise plan, seeing a financial planner, or working on your goals. Whatever the items are, the weekend will not be nearly as effective if you do not follow up on your action items.

Put your goals into action — You have now spent a weekend making wonderful plans for your future. Don't let things drop now! What is on your to-do list? Divvy these items up so each person has some follow-up responsibilities from your retreat. The division of labor doesn't have to be equal, but each person should take part in putting your work into action.

Now is the time — Take some time this afternoon to plan for the week ahead. If you spend just a few minutes reviewing your action plans and identifying which items you will put on your calendar for the week ahead, you will find that you accomplished much more this week. A weekly review of your personal and family goals is a good habit to get into.

Keep a record — Hopefully taking a retreat will become a yearly habit for you (and maybe even your family). Keep all of the information from this retreat in one central location so that in the future you can check in with ideas you had, dreams you shared, and plans you made. Did your dreams change? Did you accomplish your plans? Did your ideas pan out? Seeing that your successes are the results of conscious choices you made and well-executed planning will give you a great feeling of accomplishment.

The 60-day challenge — What did you identify on your retreat that is a *habit* you need to change or a new habit you need to start? Phillippa Lally recently published a paper in the *European Journal of Social Psychology* reporting that it takes sixty-six days (that is just about two short months) to transform an action into a habit or break an old habit. We invite you to take our 60-day challenge. (We know this is actually less than the stated sixty-six days, but we thought sixty days sounded better, and we know you're so smart that you can shave a few days off the average.)

Some may be tempted to take the 60-day challenge for multiple items on your wish list. This is akin to New Year's resolutions, when we profess that we are going to change everything in our lives, and then we look back two months later and we have made very little progress. That is because we tackled too much. Resist the urge to try to change everything at once. Pick the 60-day challenge you think will be successful. This is likely to be either a goal that is very important to you, or one that is fairly easy for you but you just haven't given it the time and energy you needed to accomplish it. Make this item your first 60-day challenge. Once you have success it will motivate you to take other 60-day challenges. To locate the steps in the 60-day challenge, stop by www.48HourRetreat.com and we'll show you the way.

Weekly meetings — If you don't have a weekly meeting with your partner, now is a great time to start. Come up with an agenda of items you want to touch base on each week (reviewing the goals you developed during your retreat is a great place to start). We review the week's schedule and deal with any childcare or taxi issues we might have, we plan our meals for the week, and we schedule any outings with friends we want to have. We can tell you that the weeks when we have our meetings we are *so much* more in sync with each other, and the weeks when we skip them we find ourselves running in different directions and doing double the work. Our meetings aren't long — maybe thirty minutes at most (usually more like fifteen to twenty minutes).

CHAPTER 24
AFTER THE RETREAT
(Is the Party Really Over?)

CHAPTER 24
AFTER THE RETREAT
(Is the Party Really Over?)

"We're so glad we've had this time together." (with liberties taken)
— *The Carol Burnett Show* theme song

OUR STORY: Results from Our Latest Retreat

We want you to know that we aren't feeding you a load of bull here. So we're putting in some of the results from our latest retreat. There were other results, but we didn't want to bore you with a really long list.

- We planned our summer road trip.

- Amanda committed to a new attitude/gratitude plan.

- We created a "call to the bullpen" approach for our parenting issues.

- Richard is going to learn golf this year.

- We're going to try in-house date nights.

- Richard's committing to more networking efforts.

- We made a plan for finishing this book and getting it published.

- We created a Boy Scouts plan for Josh.

- We plan to discuss eating better on a weekly basis.

- We listed Sunday meeting and quarterly review items.

So you spent the weekend, you did the work afterward, and you have the plans. But now you want to know what you can expect over the course of the next weeks, months, and years. "What now?" you ask.

Enjoy the fruits of your labor — We hope your weekend was successful and that you have a renewed energy and optimism in your relationship and in your lives — after all, that is the goal of your 48 hours together, right?!? So now is the time to enjoy the results of your hard work. Revel in the "new relationship smell" that might be in the air. Give your partner that extra little kiss because you actually like them now.

Be realistic — Okay, now is where we bring you back down to Earth. We know from our experience that no matter how good our retreat was, how many goals and action plans we put into place, and how much we vowed *everything* was going to change, that just isn't realistic. People aren't built that way. We can't make wholesale changes in every aspect of our lives and sustain them over the long haul (hello — need we bring up New Year's resolutions again?). But we do know from experience that you can execute *many* of the plans you made. "Which ones?" you ask. Well, that we can't tell you. But know that this is a process, and those goals and action plans are there to inspire you and guide you. And after one year you will look back and be amazed by how much you accomplished just because you had a plan in place — whether you were following it diligently or not.

Put your plans on paper — Put together your notes from the retreat. Print out your goals. Review them regularly — maybe each week at your planning meeting. Post some on the refrigerator or maybe the bathroom mirror. Just having a retreat without putting those plans in motion is pretty silly, no?

Share your results with us — We want to know how you did. We really do! Every couple that does a 48 Hour Retreat is like a couple of chicks to us. You've left our nest but we still want to know what's happening in your relationship. We want to see what beautiful paths you have in front of you. (Yes, that may sound hokey, but we have a soft underbelly too – we just don't let people see it all that often.) We want to know what your experience was like. We think about you, we pray for you, we worry about you. So let us know how it went. Don't leave us hanging, Bro!

Share your results with others — There is a whole community of 48 Hour Retreaters who want to know how you did. Join the conversation at www.48HourRetreat.com. We know that you are probably like us, and one of the main reasons we didn't do a "normal" marriage retreat is that we didn't want to share *our crap* with others. But maybe you are also like us in that once you did one (or a few), you liked the results so much that you actually wanted to share your results with others. And sometimes it is nice to get feedback from people who don't know you and aren't invested in your "stuff" — kind of an objective opinion.

Plan for your next retreat — Make a date now for your next "check-up." In six months you should get back together for a day to go over the agenda items and see what kind of progress you are making.

Think of your mini-retreat day like a middle-of-the-quarter parent-teacher conference. A "check-in," "status update" kind of retreat. While you might add in some new issues, the goal of this get-together is to pull out your notes and plans from your 48 Hour Retreat and ask each other: "How bad are we doing?" Just kidding. But do be honest. Use this as an opportunity to get back on course (if you have strayed).

Although you hope that things will stay on track, it does take a concentrated effort. Make a pledge to yourself and your partner that you will have your check-up, as well as another retreat, a year from now. Note: Unless you set really simple goals, or are even more Type A than we are, you'll probably find some areas where you've really done well and other areas where you've fallen short. Cut yourselves a break, reprioritize, recommit, and charge into the next six months with a new attitude and maybe a slightly altered set of goals. Really! It's okay. Stop fretting. Just by doing your retreat you are way ahead of where you would have been.

Change things up to keep it fresh — It is great to have consistency, but boredom breeds inaction. So from time to time reword your action plans or come up with a few new steps. Or maybe share your goals with others. Do whatever it takes to keep your goals alive and to keep yourselves motivated.

Sign up for reminders — Sometimes we all need a little nudge in the right direction. That is what *we* are here for. You can sign up for our reminder service (where else but at www.48HourRetreat.com). There you enter your goals and action plans and we send you reminders. You can decide how often, and we promise to make them sometimes witty and sometimes sarcastic.

Well, that's it, people. The book is over. But of course your journey is not. And we're not saying goodbye, we're just saying "We'll see you on the site." Because that is where you'll find us. And that is where our conversation will continue. Until then, we'll just say…

Richard: So long, farewell, Auf Weidersehen, goodbye.

Amanda: We're going to close the book with something from *The Sound of Music*?

Richard: Yep.

Amanda: Don't you want to pick something a little more current?

Richard: Nope.

Amanda: You don't want to pick something a little more hip to close out our cool/witty/sarcastic book?

Richard: Nope.

Amanda: Super-de-duper!

OUR STORY: Did You Think I Could Resist? (Amanda's Take)

I just couldn't pass up one last opportunity to tell you a personal story. (Yes, indulge me. I love these boxes, and I also love emotional closure!)

As you know by now, I have been a meeting planner by profession for many years. There is an interesting dynamic that happens at conferences. They are very intense experiences where the organizers work endless hours and usually get little sleep, all to make a special experience for the people attending the meeting. If done correctly the meeting can produce a magical experience for everyone involved. And what I have found is that the staffs that work these events often form deep and strong bonds.

Working a conference is kinda like having gone to war together (not to downplay the experiences of our fine men and women who actually serve our country and go to war). Your experience was very intense and special. But then you come home to real life, and you want to tell your loved ones about it and have them understand how special your bonds are. And yet you have a hard time because they weren't there and the bonding is hard to put into words.

Well, our retreats are often like that. Richard and I share struggles and experiences on our retreats that bond us together. We come back with a fresh attitude and spirit renewed. And when people ask us what happened we have a hard time identifying exactly what made it so special. But in the end we just know that it works. And we hope it has worked for you, too!

SECTION 5
Other Stuff

Acknowledgements
(A Big Heaping Helping of Thank Yous)

We wanted to start out with a big steaming pile of thank yous to all of the wonderful people who helped make this book happen. But along with these thanks must go the apologies, because this list will no doubt be incomplete. We only have limited space, and quite frankly this isn't a book about thank yous. So this really can't go on too long.

If you are reading this page and don't see your name here, please don't be upset (because let's face it…you aren't reading this unless you think your name might be here). This project was so much bigger than we ever could have imagined, and we never could have done it without all of the people involved at every turn.

There are so many who supported us and encouraged us along this journey that we are *bound* to leave someone out. So if you are the person who is reading this looking for your name and you don't find it, please come up and smack us on the side of our heads. And then we will give you a very personal thank you.

Now here goes our attempt to remember those who have made this all possible:

First and foremost, thank you to God. This is really His book, and we are only the messengers. We appreciate that He has entrusted us with this important mission, and we will do all that we can to fulfill the mission that He has given us.

Almost right up there is thanks to our parents. You have provided the most important component to our success — amazing examples. We are truly blessed to have amazing parents who have shown us what successful relationships look like. You have lived lives that are truly *proactive*, and have always told us (and shown us) that we could do and be whatever we wanted to be. If we are risk-takers, thinkers, and doers, it is because you allowed us to be so and supported us when we wanted to go there. Special thanks to Carol for her transcribing, proofing, listening, and just good life advice that laid the foundation for much of this book.

To our family who encouraged us and actually did work on this project: Steven — thank you for graphic design help and solid business advice. And it never ceased to amaze us when our eight- and eleven-year-old children were encouraging, interested, and supportive. We do this for you, and we hope we make you proud. Joshua and Carli — you are the best gifts that God could ever have given us.

To Barb — Amanda's muse, constant companion, and encourager throughout this whole process — I have *no doubt* that this book would never have come to completion if it weren't for you.

To Jane, Megan, and Lori — your creativity and intelligence have added so much to our whole project. Thank you for being such great contributors to our success.

To our village — we said it in these pages, but it bears repeating. Without you, life would be so much less sweet and so much less fun. We wouldn't be able to do what we do without you. Some of you are in these pages by name, and though many of you go unnamed, you continue to support and love us. Thank you!

To our friends — you are the best support system we could have. Thank you for your encouragement and love. We are thrilled to have you along for the ride. But now, we expect you to get to work and make this thing a huge success!!!

To Clint and Carrie — for being our very first guinea pigs and for being so generous with your time and talents.

To all of our 48 Hour Allies — thank you for the support and for spreading the word to those who need to hear it.

To Rosemary who nurtured us along this journey — you had a vision for our project bigger than we had when we started, and we will be forever grateful to you for all that you gave us.

To Lynne and Gwen and the team at Love Your Life Publishing — thank you for taking our written words and making them come to life.

As of press time, some particular people who contributed their ideas or work on the whole project are:

Carol Adams	Malinda Marcus
Don Adams	Jeffrey Mauro
Steven Adams	Eva Naccari
Dewey Barnes	Laura Norvell
Dick Barney	Phil Piga
Marilyn Barney	Brigette Polmar
Gigi Blair	Carrie Quisenberry
Robyn Goldman	Clint Quisenberry
Melody Heavner	Jane Rothschilds
Barb Herod	Julie Simmons
Dave Herod	Shannan Slovon
Michael Holstein	Lori Teachum
Megan Johnson	Mark Wilkinson
Bill Liggett	and Tim (yep, you made it in)

About the Authors

(Our publisher made us write this — we hate talking about ourselves — HA! Yeah, right!)

Richard was born in Fairbanks, Alaska. Yup. Let that sink in for a minute. While he didn't grow up in an igloo, he did go through the life-changing trauma of seeing a first-grade classmate get his tongue stuck to the metal swing set in the winter! Richard managed to escape the frigid climes of Alaska for the relatively balmy weather of Western Montana, where all his formative years occurred. Having a forester for a dad meant Boy Scouts, hunting, hiking, canoeing, etc.

Missoula, Montana was a great place to grow up, but the lure of other adventures pulled Richard to Bucknell University where he graduated with a bachelor's degree in human resource management — a degree he made up! Anyhow, Richard then headed out into the cold cruel world of business in the Washington, DC area, where he found his passion for sales, marketing, leading, and coaching new young leaders. He helped start a small company that grew to fifty-plus employees before being sold, and was instrumental in the growth of several other companies.

Oh yeah, along the way he met this crazy redhead and got married! Richard returned to school just before children entered his life and secured a master's degree in marketing from Johns Hopkins. Throughout his career, Richard has been an avid reader of books and articles on management, leadership, marketing, and most other business topics. He's sort of a leadership junkie (not flattering, but true).

When he's not hauling his kids to baseball, soccer, swimming, dance, or other events, he enjoys golfing (sort of), all outdoor activities, following politics, and watching most sports, but especially cheering on his Miami Dolphins, Washington Nationals, and Washington Capitals. Richard's parents have been married for fifty-two years and counting!

Amanda was born in a hardscrabble town just outside Pittsburgh, Pennsylvania, which doesn't explain at all her expensive tastes. It does however explain how she acquired a love of motorcycle sports (motocross, hare scrambles, etc.) and learned at an early age how to lift the gas can to re-fuel her dad's bike during a race. As a child she was an active member in the marching band and a ringleader in get-togethers that often ended up back at her parents' twenty-acre property.

After graduating from the mighty Penn-Trafford High School (really not all that noteworthy), Amanda headed for the big city of Washington, DC and American University. Besides her endless hours as president of the Residences Hall Association, Amanda also managed to squeeze in a few classes, allowing her to graduate with a bachelor's degree in international business. After a couple of jobs in meeting planning, and agreeing to marry Richard (out of pity, of course), Amanda took the plunge and started her own meeting-planning and event-management company which she has successfully run for fifteen years.

As the CEO of the family (Chief Entertainment Officer), Amanda takes her job seriously and has been the driving force in keeping fun in the marriage. While maintaining her roots as a rabid Steelers fan, Amanda has slowly been converted over to a Capitals and Nationals fan, but more importantly a screaming fan of any team her kids are playing on. She loves to sit and knit for hours — NOT! Actually, she loves to socialize with friends, go to shows, and, as her dad likes to say, "get out and experience life!" And since they're a bit younger, Amanda's parents have been married for a mere forty-seven years.

A friend recently pointed out to Richard and Amanda that they very closely resemble Marshall and Lilly from the TV show, *How I Met Your Mother*. After they were done laughing hysterically, Richard and Amanda had to admit that they agreed. And if you've seen the show, now you know who they are.

Oh yeah, plus their relationship truly is legend...wait for it...dary.